# The Healthy
# Air Fryer Cookbook UK

1900 Days Affordable and Flavorful Air Fryer Recipes using UK measurements for Beginners | Favorites for Side Dishes, Desserts, and Snacks, Incl.

*Jayne J. Tovar*

## Copyright© 2023 By Jayne J. Tovar
## All Rights Reserved

This book is copyright protected. It is only for personal use.
You cannot amend, distribute, sell, use,
quote or paraphrase any part of the content within this book,
without the consent of the author or publisher.
Under no circumstances will any blame or
legal responsibility be held against the publisher,
or author, for any damages, reparation,
or monetary loss due to the information contained within this book,
either directly or indirectly.

**Disclaimer Notice:**

Please note the information contained within this
document is for educational and entertainment purposes only.
All effort has been executed to present accurate,
up to date, reliable, complete information.
No warranties of any kind are declared or implied.
Readers acknowledge that the author is not engaged
in the rendering of legal,
financial, medical or professional advice.
The content within this book has been derived from various sources.
Please consult a licensed professional before attempting any
techniques outlined in this book.
By reading this document,
the reader agrees that under no circumstances is the
author responsible for any losses,
direct or indirect,
that are incurred as a result of the use of the
information contained within this document, including,
but not limited to, errors, omissions, or inaccuracies.

# Contents

## Introduction .................................................................................................. 1

What Are Air Fryers? ............................ 1
How to Choose an Air Fryer? ..................... 2
What Can You Cook in an Air Fryer and What Foods to Avoid? ................................. 3
The Benefits of Air Fryers ....................... 4
Cleaning and Maintaining Your Air Fryer ...... 4
Care Tips for Your Air Fryer .................... 5
Frequently Asked Questions .................... 6

## Chapter 1: Breakfast ..................................................................................... 7

Air-Fried Breakfast Tacos with Cheesy Hash Brown Shell ..................................... 7
Banana Nutella Stuffed French Toast Bites ... 7
Air-Fried Blueberry Lemon Ricotta Pancake Poppers ........................................... 7
Sweet Potato and Bacon Breakfast Empanadas 8
Cinnamon Roll Apple Fritters with Cream Cheese Drizzle .................................... 8
Air-Fried Eggs in Avocado Toast Cups ......... 9
Breakfast Sausage and Cheese Stuffed Crescent Rolls ............................................ 9
Lemon Poppy Seed Air-Fried Donut Holes ... 9
Air-Fried Breakfast Quesadillas with Ham and Pineapple ........................................... 10
Crunchy Cereal-Coated Air-Fried French Toast Sticks ............................................ 10
Spinach and Feta Egg Cups with Sun-Dried Tomatoes .............................................. 10
Air-Fried Peanut Butter and Jelly Wontons ... 11
Churro-Style Air-Fried Waffles with Chocolate Dipping Sauce ................................... 11
Cheesy Spinach and Artichoke Stuffed Breakfast Mushrooms ..................................... 11
Raspberry Coconut Almond Granola Bars ...... 12
Air-Fried Breakfast Sushi with Banana and Nut Butter ............................................ 12
Greek Yoghurt and Mixed Berry Parfait Cups 12
Air-Fried Quinoa and Veggie Breakfast Bites 12
Ham and Cheese Stuffed Pretzel Bites ......... 13
Savoury Breakfast Egg Rolls with Sausage and Veggies ............................................ 13
Raspberry Chocolate Chip Air-Fried Muffins... 14
Matcha Green Tea Pancake Bites ............... 14
Apple Cinnamon Breakfast Egg Rolls ......... 14
Air Fryer Breakfast Sausage Patties ............ 15
Air Fryer Banana Bread .......................... 15
Air Fryer Breakfast Hash ........................ 15
Air Fryer Avocado Toast ......................... 15
Cheesy Bell Pepper Eggs ........................ 16
Cheddar Eggs ..................................... 16
Homemade Cherry Breakfast Tarts ............. 16

## Chapter 2: Fish and Seafood ....................................................................... 17

Crispy Coconut Shrimp with Pineapple Dipping Sauce .................................... 17
Cajun-Style Air-Fried Catfish Nuggets ......... 17
Zesty Lemon Herb Air-Fried Scallops ......... 17
Spicy Sriracha Honey Glazed Air-Fried Salmon 18
Garlic Butter Parmesan Air-Fried Shrimp ...... 18
Mediterranean Herb-Stuffed Air-Fried Calamari Rings ................................... 18
Crispy Cajun Crab Cakes with Remoulade Sauce ............................................... 18
Crispy Coconut Lime Air-Fried Oysters ......... 19
Buffalo-Style Air-Fried Popcorn Shrimp ...... 19

Garlic and Herb Air-Fried Lobster Tails ......... 20
Tandoori-Style Air-Fried Shrimp Tikka ......... 20
Lemon Herb Air-Fried Scampi with Linguine  20
Coconut Curry Air-Fried Mussels ................ 21
Jerk-Spiced Air-Fried Red Snapper ............ 21
Almond-Crusted Air-Fried Halibut Steaks ...... 21
Chipotle Lime Air-Fried Fish Tacos ............ 21
Cajun Seafood Stuffed Eggplant Boats ......... 22

Garlic and Sesame Air-Fried Soft Shell Crab ... 22
Chimichurri Grilled Shrimp Skewers ............ 23
Crispy Cornmeal Air-Fried Catfish Po' Boys ... 23
Caribbean-Style Air-Fried Conch Fritters ...... 23
Black Sesame-Crusted Air-Fried Ahi Tuna Sliders ... 24
Classic Fish & Chips ............................. 24
Fish Gratin ...................................... 25
Crunchy Fish Sticks ............................. 25

## Chapter 3: Poultry ............................................................. 26

Buffalo Chicken Egg Rolls with Blue Cheese Dip 26
Chimichurri Lime Air-Fried Chicken Thighs ... 26
Korean BBQ Air-Fried Chicken Wings .......... 26
Stuffed Pesto and Mozzarella Air-Fried Chicken Breasts................................................ 27
Coconut Curry Air-Fried Chicken Skewers ... 27
Honey Mustard Pretzel-Crusted Air-Fried Chicken Bites .............................................. 27
Jerk-Spiced Air-Fried Turkey Meatballs......... 28
Garlic Herb Butter Air-Fried Cornish Hens ... 28
Greek Yoghurt and Herb Marinated Air-Fried Turkey Cutlets....................................... 28
Maple Sriracha Glazed Air-Fried Duck Breast  29
Panko-Crusted Air-Fried Chicken Cordon Bleu 29
Ranch and Bacon Air-Fried Chicken Sliders ... 29
Hawaiian Pineapple Teriyaki Air-Fried Chicken Skewers .............................................. 30

Lemon Dill Air-Fried Chicken Schnitzel ...... 30
Spinach and Feta Stuffed Air-Fried Chicken Rolls 30
Cajun Sweet Potato Air-Fried Chicken Bites ... 31
BBQ Pulled Chicken Air-Fried Sweet Potato Skins ................................................. 31
Mediterranean Herb Air-Fried Quail with Olives and Feta ............................................. 32
Thai Red Curry Air-Fried Chicken Lettuce Wraps ................................................ 32
Rosemary and Garlic Air-Fried Chicken Legs  32
Cranberry and Brie Stuffed Air-Fried Chicken Breasts................................................ 33
Spicy Honey Lime Air-Fried Chicken Wings ... 33
Kentucky Air Fried Chicken Wings ............ 33
Buttermilk-Fried Drumsticks .................... 34
Sriracha-Honey Chicken Nuggets ............... 34
Air Fryer Chicken-Fried Steak .................. 34

## Chapter 4: Beef, Pork & Lamb ..................................................... 35

Korean BBQ Air-Fried Beef Bulgogi Sliders ... 35
Crispy Garlic Parmesan Air-Fried Pork Tenderloin Medallions ......................................... 35
Moroccan Spiced Air-Fried Lamb Meatballs ... 35
Teriyaki Pineapple Air-Fried Beef Skewers ... 36
BBQ Pulled Pork-Stuffed Air-Fried Jalapenos  36
Rosemary and Garlic Air-Fried Lamb Chops ... 36
Tex-Mex Air-Fried Beef Taquitos with Avocado Dip 37
Italian Herb Air-Fried Pork Milanese ............ 37
Spicy Szechuan Air-Fried Beef Stir-Fry ......... 37
Mediterranean Stuffed Air-Fried Lamb Burgers  38
Honey Mustard Glazed Air-Fried Pork Belly Bites 38

Mongolian-Style Air-Fried Beef and Broccoli  38
Greek Lemon Garlic Air-Fried Lamb Chops ... 39
Jamaican Jerk Air-Fried Pork Ribs ............... 39
Spinach and Feta Stuffed Air-Fried Beef Roll-Ups 39
Apricot Glazed Air-Fried Lamb Steaks ......... 40
Panko-Crusted Air-Fried Pork Schnitzel......... 40
Mexican Street Corn Air-Fried Beef Tacos...... 40
Cajun Butter Air-Fried Beef and Potato Wedges 41
Mediterranean Lamb Gyro Meatballs with Tzatziki Sauce 41
Bacon-Wrapped Pork Tenderloin ............... 42
Beef Haslet (meatloaf) ........................... 42
Parmesan Herb Filet Mignon ..................... 42

## Chapter 5: Beans & Legumes .................................................. 43

- Crispy Cajun Chickpea Snack Mix............... 43
- Buffalo Ranch Air-Fried Edamame............... 43
- Za'atar Spiced Air-Fried Falafel Bites........... 43
- Tex-Mex Air-Fried Black Bean Quesadillas ... 43
- Spicy Curry Air-Fried Lentil Samosas ......... 44
- Garlic Parmesan Air-Fried Green Bean Fries ... 44
- Mediterranean Herb Air-Fried Fava Bean Hummus .................................................. 44
- BBQ Ranch Air-Fried Soybeans (Roasted Corn Nuts) 45
- Cinnamon Sugar Air-Fried Sweet Potato Hummus Dipper Chips ............................................. 45
- Everything Bagel Seasoned Air-Fried Chickpeas 45
- Thai Red Curry Air-Fried Red Lentil Patties ... 46
- Chili Lime Air-Fried Split Peas ................... 46
- Indian Spiced Air-Fried Masala Vada (Lentil Fritters) 46
- Truffle Rosemary Air-Fried Pinto Beans......... 46
- Za'atar Spiced Air-Fried Broad Beans ......... 47
- Greek Herb Air-Fried Gigante Beans ............ 47
- Coconut Curry Air-Fried Chana Chaat ......... 47
- Spicy Ranch Air-Fried Lentil Crunchies......... 47
- Moroccan Harissa Air-Fried Chickpea Croquettes 48
- Cheesy Garlic Air-Fried Cannellini Beans ...... 48
- Crispy Chili Lime Air-Fried Black Bean Tostones 48
- Spinach and Feta Stuffed Air-Fried Mung Bean Paratha.................................................. 49
- Hawaiian Pineapple Teriyaki Air-Fried Butter Beans .................................................. 49
- Simple Air Fried Crispy Brussels Sprouts ...... 49

## Chapter 6: Healthy Vegetables .................................................. 50

- Crispy Courgette Parmesan Fries ............... 50
- Buffalo Cauliflower Bites with Blue Cheese Dip 50
- Lemon Herb Air-Fried Asparagus Spears ...... 50
- Coconut Curry Air-Fried Brussels Sprouts ...... 50
- Garlic Parmesan Air-Fried Broccoli Florets ... 51
- Pesto and Mozzarella Air-Fried Portobello Mushrooms 51
- Spicy Sriracha Air-Fried Green Beans ......... 51
- Lemon Rosemary Air-Fried Artichoke Hearts 52
- Crispy Turmeric Air-Fried Okra ................... 52
- Greek Yoghurt and Herb Marinated Air-Fried Veggie Kebabs ......................................... 52
- Ranch and Bacon Air-Fried Cauliflower Tots... 52
- Teriyaki Glazed Air-Fried Bok Choy ............ 53
- Italian Herb Air-Fried Tomato Bruschetta ...... 53
- Sweet Potato and Black Bean Air-Fried Taquitos 53
- Sesame Ginger Air-Fried Snow Peas ............ 54
- Balsamic Glazed Air-Fried Beet Chips ......... 54
- Moroccan Spiced Air-Fried Carrot Falafel ...... 54
- Zesty Lemon Dill Air-Fried Cabbage Wedges 54
- Indian Spiced Air-Fried Okra Pakoras ......... 55
- Spinach and Feta Stuffed Air-Fried Portobello Caps 55
- Turmeric Cauliflower Rice Air-Fried Fritters ... 55
- Cumin and Paprika Air-Fried Butternut Squash Cubes 56
- Spicy Ranch Air-Fried Green Bean Fries ...... 56
- Coconut Lime Air-Fried Sweet Potato Medallions 56
- Hawaiian Pineapple Teriyaki Air-Fried Vegetable Skewers .................................................. 56
- Air Fryer Roasted Brussels Sprouts with Balsamic Glaze 57
- Air-fried stuffed peppers with quinoa and vegetables 57
- Air-fried Brussels sprouts with bacon ......... 57

## Chapter 7: Rice and Pasta .................................................. 58

- Crispy Parmesan Garlic Air-Fried Risotto Balls 58
- Pesto and Mozzarella Air-Fried Arancini ...... 58
- Lemon Herb Air-Fried Orzo with Roasted Vegetables ............................................. 58
- Coconut Curry Air-Fried Vegetable Fried Rice 58
- Stuffed Italian Air-Fried Peppers with Tomato Rice 59
- Teriyaki Glazed Air-Fried Pineapple Rice ...... 59
- Cheesy Garlic Air-Fried Gnocchi with Pesto ... 59
- Moroccan Spiced Air-Fried Cauliflower Rice Pilaf 60
- Buffalo Cauliflower and Blue Cheese Air-Fried Macaroni Cups ......................................... 60
- Coconut Lime Air-Fried Jasmine Rice Balls ... 60

## Chapter 8: Appetisers and Snacks ... 61

Coconut Curry Air-Fried Brussels Sprouts ...... 61
Crispy Carrot Parmesan Fries ..................... 61
Lemon Herb Air-Fried Asparagus Spears ...... 61
Cajun Shrimp and Sausage Air-Fried Jambalaya Bites 61
Mediterranean Stuffed Air-Fried Grape Leaves 62
Pesto and Mozzarella Air-Fried Arancini ...... 62
Tex-Mex Air-Fried Chicken and Rice Taquitos 62
Spinach and Feta Stuffed Air-Fried Portobello Caps 63
Zesty Lemon Dill Air-Fried Cabbage Wedges 63
Hawaiian Pineapple Teriyaki Air-Fried Butter Beans 63
Garlic Parmesan Air-Fried Green Bean Fries ... 64
Indian Spiced Air-Fried Okra Pakoras ......... 64
Ranch and Bacon Air-Fried Cauliflower Tots ... 64
Lemon Rosemary Air-Fried Artichoke Hearts 65
Buffalo Cauliflower and Blue Cheese Air-Fried Macaroni Cups ..................... 65
Coconut Lime Air-Fried Sweet Potato Medallions 65
Stuffed Italian Air-Fried Peppers with Tomato Rice 65
Moroccan Spiced Air-Fried Carrot Falafel ...... 66
Caprese Air-Fried Ravioli Skewers............... 66
Balsamic Glazed Air-Fried Beet Chips ......... 66
Cajun Air-Fried Black Eyed Peas ............... 67
Lemon Poppy Seed Air-Fried Donut Holes ... 67
Crispy Parmesan Garlic Air-Fried Risotto Balls 67
Indian Spiced Air-Fried Lentil Samosas ......... 68
Hawaiian Pineapple Teriyaki Air-Fried Rice Crackers 68

## Chapter 9: Desserts ... 69

Cinnamon Sugar Air-Fried Apple Fritters ...... 69
S'mores Air-Fried Empanadas..................... 69
Red Velvet Air-Fried Whoopie Pies ............ 69
Raspberry Coconut Almond Granola Bars ...... 70
Matcha Green Tea Air-Fried Macarons ......... 70
Cheesecake-Stuffed Air-Fried Strawberries ... 71
Mini Berry Galettes with Air-Fried Crusts ...... 71
Blueberry Lemon Air-Fried Pound Cake Bites 72
Oreo Air-Fried Cake Pops ....................... 72
Chocolate Chip Cookie Dough Air-Fried Egg Rolls ................................................. 72
Pineapple Coconut Air-Fried Spring Rolls ...... 72
Chai Spiced Air-Fried Rice Pudding Cups ...... 73
Blackberry Lavender Air-Fried Tarts ............ 73
Mint Chocolate Chip Air-Fried Ice Cream Bites 74
Caramelized Banana Air-Fried Chimichangas 74
Cannoli Air-Fried Wonton Cups .................. 74
Caramel Popcorn Air-Fried Cake ............... 75
Strawberry Shortcake Air-Fried Napoleons ... 75
Cinnamon Apple Air-Fried Samosas ............ 75
Raspberry White Chocolate Air-Fried Turnovers ................................................. 76

# Introduction

I am thrilled to share my passion for cooking and the incredible possibilities that the versatile air fryer offers. Within these pages, you will find a delightful collection of easy-to-follow recipes to make the most out of your air fryer.

Cooking has always been a personal and intimate experience for me, allowing me to express creativity, nurture loved ones, and explore new flavours. I firmly believe that regardless of your culinary background, preparing delicious meals can bring joy and satisfaction to both the cook and diners.

As a fellow home cook, I understand the challenges and hesitations that come with trying out new recipes or using a new kitchen appliance. Therefore, this cookbook is tailored specifically for beginners. Whether you are an experienced chef curious about air frying or a novice cook stepping into the kitchen for the first time, this book is here to guide you every step of the way.

I want you to know that you are not alone on this culinary adventure. Throughout this cookbook, I will be your companion, sharing my knowledge, tips, and personal experiences to help you navigate the world of air frying with confidence and ease. My goal is to empower and excite you to try new recipes, experiment with flavours, and create delicious meals for yourself, your family, and your friends.

Inside these pages, you will discover a variety of recipes that showcase the versatility of the air fryer. From crispy appetisers to mouthwatering mains, and even indulgent desserts, there is something to delight every palate. You will be amazed at how the air fryer can transform your favourite dishes into healthier versions without compromising on flavour or texture.

So, whether you need a quick weeknight dinner, plan to host a gathering with friends, or simply want to satisfy your cravings, this cookbook is your go-to guide for unlocking the full potential of your air fryer. Get ready to embark on a culinary journey filled with tantalising aromas, delightful flavours, and the joy of creating memorable meals.

Always remember, cooking is a delightful adventure that encourages exploration, creativity, and, above all, enjoyment. I encourage you to embrace this journey, make it your own, and have fun along the way. Let's dive in and discover the incredible possibilities that await you in the world of air frying!

## What Are Air Fryers?

Do you ever dream of savouring your favourite crispy, fried delicacies guilt-free and without the mess of traditional deep frying? Enter the groundbreaking kitchen appliance that's taking the culinary world by storm: the air fryer! If you're curious about the magic behind air fryers and how they work, you've come to the right place. Let's delve into the captivating world of air fryers.

At first glance, an air fryer may resemble a compact countertop oven, but it offers so much more. It's a game-changer for anyone seeking to relish delicious, crispy dishes with a fraction of the oil and clean-up hassle. By utilising hot air circulation combined with a minimal amount of oil, air fryers deliver that coveted crispy texture on the outside while preserving moisture and perfectly cooking the food inside.

o, how does it work? Inside the air fryer, you'll find a powerful heating element and a high-speed fan. Set your desired temperature and time, and the heating element swiftly warms the air inside the fryer, while the fan circulates this hot air around the food. This circulating air creates a convection effect, simulating the frying process, but with significantly reduced oil usage.

An outstanding advantage of air fryers is their ability to cook food evenly and rapidly. The hot air reaches every nook and cranny of the ingredients, ensuring uniform cooking and achieving that appealing golden-brown finish. Enjoy crispy French fries, crunchy chicken wings, or flaky pastries without the need for excessive oil or lengthy frying times.

Yet, air fryers are not just limited to frying. They excel in baking, roasting, grilling, and reheating leftovers. From beautifully roasted vegetables to succulent grilled meats, the possibilities are boundless. Their remarkable versatility makes them a prized addition to any kitchen.

Aside from convenience and versatility, air fryers boast significant health benefits. With little to no oil, air fryers dramatically reduce the calorie and fat content of your favourite fried foods. This means you can relish guilt-free versions of your beloved crispy treats without compromising on taste and texture.

Moreover, air fryers provide a cleaner and more hassle-free cooking experience. Say goodbye to greasy splatters and lingering frying odours. Air fryers are designed to contain the mess and keep your kitchen tidy. Many models even have dishwasher-safe parts, simplifying clean-up.

Whether you prioritise health, are a busy parent, or love to experiment with new cooking techniques, an air fryer is a superb addition to your kitchen arsenal. It's a tool that brings convenience, flavour, and healthier alternatives to your beloved dishes.

In summary, air fryers are innovative appliances that use hot air circulation and minimal oil to achieve crispy, flavorful results. They offer a healthier alternative to deep frying and provide versatility in cooking a wide range of dishes. With an air fryer, you can indulge in your favourite fried foods guilt-free, with less mess and hassle. So, get ready to elevate your cooking game and relish the delights of crispy perfection with the magic of air frying!

## How to Choose an Air Fryer?

Selecting the ideal air fryer for your kitchen may seem overwhelming due to the abundance of options available in the market. However, fear not! We're here to walk you through the process and assist you in finding the air fryer that perfectly aligns with your needs and culinary aspirations. Let's delve into the key factors to consider when choosing your ultimate air fryer.

- **Capacity**: The first crucial aspect to ponder is the air fryer's capacity. Take into account the size of your household and the amount of food you typically cook. Air fryers come in various sizes, ranging from compact models with around 2 litres of capacity to larger ones capable of holding 6 litres or more. For larger families or frequent entertainers, a larger capacity might be more suitable, while a smaller capacity can suffice if you have limited kitchen space or cook for one or two people.
- **Power and Cooking Performance**: The power of an air fryer is measured in watts, and it directly impacts its cooking performance. Higher wattage translates to faster cooking times and more efficient heat circulation. Look for models with at least 1500 watts for optimal results, ensuring even cooking and achieving that desired crispiness in a shorter time.
- **Temperature Range and Controls**: Check the temperature range offered by the air fryer. Most models offer a range of 180°C to 200°C, suitable for a wide variety of recipes. However, if you enjoy experimenting with various cooking techniques, opt for models that provide a broader temperature range. Additionally, consider the ease of use and controls. Some air fryers feature digital displays and pre-set cooking programs, simplifying the process of selecting the desired temperature and cooking time.
- **Additional Features:** Air fryers often boast a range of additional features to enhance your cooking experience. Some models include built-in timers, adjustable cooking racks, or even multiple cooking functions like baking and grilling. Evaluate which features are important to you and align with your cooking preferences. For instance, if you enjoy

baking, look for an air fryer that offers baking capabilities.
- **Ease of Cleaning:** Nobody wants to spend hours scrubbing and cleaning after a delightful meal. Thus, consider the ease of cleaning when selecting an air fryer. Look for models with non-stick cooking surfaces, removable and dishwasher-safe parts, and accessible nooks and crannies that are easy to wipe clean. This will save you time and effort in maintaining your air fryer.
- **Brand and Reviews**: Lastly, it's always prudent to research the brand and read customer reviews. Seek reputable brands with a proven track record of producing quality appliances. Customer reviews offer valuable insights into the performance, durability, and overall satisfaction of the air fryer you're considering.

By taking these factors into account, you can narrow down your options and discover the air fryer that best suits your needs and preferences. Remember to keep your cooking habits, kitchen space, and desired features in mind. So, prepare yourself for a flavorful journey and elevate your cooking experience with the perfect air fryer companion!

## What Can You Cook in an Air Fryer and What Foods to Avoid?

The versatility of an air fryer is truly extraordinary, offering you the ability to cook a wide range of foods with minimal oil and a delectable, crispy finish. Whether you're a daring culinary explorer or a fan of comfort food, the possibilities are boundless. Let's embark on a journey to explore the various dishes you can create in an air fryer and also take note of some foods that may not be ideal for this cooking method.

- **Crispy Delights:** Air fryers excel at producing crispy delights without the need for excessive oil. You can relish golden and crunchy French fries, onion rings, chicken wings, mozzarella sticks, and even breaded fish or shrimp. The hot air circulating around the food ensures a satisfying crunch while reducing the guilt associated with deep-fried indulgences.
- **Roasted Vegetables**: Roasting vegetables in an air fryer is a game-changer. It enhances their natural sweetness and caramelization, resulting in perfectly roasted Brussels sprouts, cauliflower florets, sweet potato fries, or even a medley of vibrant peppers. Simply toss the vegetables with a little oil and your choice of seasonings, and let the air fryer work its magic.
- **Grilled Meats and Seafood**: Yes, it's true! You can achieve that mouthwatering char-grilled flavour on meats and seafood in an air fryer. Marinate chicken drumsticks or skewered kebabs, place them in the air fryer, and let the intense heat create a delightful sear. From juicy steaks and grilled salmon fillets to succulent shrimp or pork chops, the air fryer can deliver satisfying grill-like results.
- **Baked Goods:** Air fryers are not limited to savoury dishes. You can also bake a variety of goods, from muffins and cupcakes to cinnamon rolls and even small cakes. The hot air circulates evenly, ensuring a fluffy and perfectly baked outcome. So, satisfy your sweet tooth with healthier alternatives to traditional baking methods.

While the air fryer offers a world of culinary possibilities, there are a few foods to avoid or use with caution:

- **Wet Batters**: Foods with wet batters, such as tempura or thick pancake batters, may not yield desirable results in an air fryer. The excess moisture can make the food soggy instead of crispy. If you're craving a dish with a wet batter, it's best to stick to traditional deep-frying methods.
- **Delicate Foods:** Delicate foods that require gentle cooking, like flaky fish fillets or tender vegetables, may not fare well in an air fryer. The intense heat and circulating air might cause these foods to become overcooked or dry. It's important to monitor and adjust cooking times accordingly to prevent

overcooking.
- **Foods with High Water Content:** Foods with high water content, such as grapes, watery fruits, or leafy greens, are not suitable for air frying. The high moisture content can result in uneven cooking and a less desirable texture. These foods are best enjoyed fresh or prepared using other cooking methods.

Remember, experimentation is key when using an air fryer. Don't be afraid to try new recipes and adapt traditional ones to suit the air fryer's cooking style. With a bit of creativity, you'll discover endless ways to make healthier, flavorful, and crispy meals using this fantastic kitchen appliance.

## The Benefits of Air Fryers

Air fryers have taken the culinary world by storm, completely transforming how we prepare our favourite dishes. These innovative kitchen appliances offer a healthier and more convenient alternative to traditional deep frying methods, making them an essential addition to any kitchen. Let's delve into the advantages of using an air fryer and discover how they can elevate your cooking experience.
- **Healthier Cooking:** One of the primary benefits of air fryers is their ability to cook food with minimal oil. Unlike traditional deep frying that requires submerging food in hot oil, air fryers use hot air circulation to cook dishes, significantly reducing the need for oil. As a result, your favourite meals become healthier, with lower fat and calorie content, without compromising on taste.
- **Reduced Fat and Calories:** By using less oil, air fryers allow you to enjoy crispy and delicious foods with reduced fat and calorie content. For example, air-fried French fries contain up to 75% less fat compared to their deep-fried counterparts. This reduction in unhealthy fats contributes to weight management and supports a healthier lifestyle.
- **Crispy and Delicious Results**: Despite using minimal oil, air fryers achieve that desirable crispy texture that we all love in fried foods. The rapid air circulation creates a convection effect, quickly heating the food's surface for a crispy exterior while retaining moisture for tender and juicy interiors. From crispy chicken wings to perfectly roasted vegetables, air fryers deliver exceptional texture and flavour.
- **Faster Cooking Time**: Air fryers are renowned for their speed and efficiency. The intense heat and even distribution of hot air lead to faster cooking

times compared to traditional ovens or stovetop methods. This time-saving benefit is perfect for busy individuals and families who want quick and tasty meals.
- **Versatility:** Air fryers are incredibly versatile, capable of cooking a wide range of dishes. From appetisers and main courses to desserts and baked goods, air fryers can handle it all. They can grill, roast, bake, and reheat leftovers, eliminating the need for multiple cooking tools and simplifying your kitchen setup.
- **Easy to Use and Clean**: Air fryers are designed with user-friendliness in mind, making them ideal for cooks of all levels. Most models feature intuitive digital controls, pre-set cooking functions, and adjustable temperature settings, allowing you to customise your cooking experience easily. Moreover, the non-stick surfaces and dishwasher-safe parts ensure effortless cleaning.
- **Safer Alternative**: Compared to traditional deep frying, air fryers offer a safer cooking method. With no open pots or pans filled with scorching oil, the risk of oil splatters and burns is significantly reduced. Air fryers also come with safety features like automatic shut-off and cool-touch handles, providing added peace of mind.

Overall, air fryers offer a plethora of benefits that make them an invaluable tool in any kitchen. From promoting healthier cooking and reducing fat intake to delivering crispy and delightful results, faster cooking times, versatility, ease of use, and enhanced safety, air fryers have revolutionised how we enjoy our favourite foods. Embrace this innovative cooking technology to create mouthwatering dishes that satiate your cravings while fostering a healthier lifestyle.

## Cleaning and Maintaining Your Air Fryer

To ensure your air fryer operates at its best and remains durable, regular cleaning is essential. Cleaning not only maintains its efficiency but also eliminates odours and prevents the accumulation of grease and residue. Follow these simple steps to clean and maintain your air fryer:
- **Unplug and Allow to Cool:** Before cleaning, always unplug the air fryer and let it cool completely. This ensures safety while handling the appliance.
- **Remove Removable Parts**: Most air fryers have parts that are dishwasher-safe or require handwashing. Check your manufacturer's instructions for specific guidelines. Typically, the frying basket, drip tray, and other accessories are removable. Detach these parts carefully for cleaning.
- **Dishwasher or Handwash:** If the parts are dishwasher-safe, place them in the dishwasher for easy cleaning. Otherwise, handwash them using warm, soapy water. Gently scrub away any residue or grease with a soft sponge or cloth. Rinse thoroughly and let them air dry or dry with a clean towel before reassembling.
- **Clean the Interior:** Use a damp cloth or sponge to wipe the interior and remove any food particles or oil. Avoid immersing the appliance in water or using abrasive cleaners that may damage the surface. For stubborn stains, mix dish soap with warm water and gently scrub the affected areas. Wipe dry with a clean cloth.
- **Address Lingering Odours: If there are lingering** odours from previous cooking, freshen up your air fryer with simple tricks. Fill the frying basket with a mixture of water and lemon juice or vinegar, then run the air fryer at a low temperature for a few minutes. Steam and acidity will help eliminate odours. Alternatively, place a small bowl of baking soda in the air fryer overnight; baking soda absorbs odours and leaves the appliance smelling fresh.
- **Clean the Exterior**: Wipe the exterior with a damp cloth to remove grease and fingerprints. For stubborn stains or residue, use a mild kitchen cleaner or a mixture of vinegar and water. Avoid abrasive materials or harsh chemicals that may damage the surface. Dry the exterior with a clean cloth to prevent water spots.
- **Regular Maintenance:** Perform regular maintenance to keep your air fryer in optimal condition. Inspect the power cord for damage, keep the air vents clear for proper ventilation, and periodically check for loose screws or other mechanical issues. Refer to your manufacturer's instructions for specific maintenance recommendations.

By following these cleaning and maintenance tips, you can enjoy your air fryer for years to come. A clean and well-maintained appliance not only ensures delicious and healthy meals but also creates a safe and pleasant cooking environment. Dedicate a little time to caring for your air fryer, and it will reward you with exceptional performance and culinary delights.

## Care Tips for Your Air Fryer

Maintaining your air fryer properly is vital for its longevity and top-notch performance. By adhering to these care tips, you can ensure that your appliance continues to deliver delectable and wholesome meals for years to come:

- **Read the Instruction Manual**: Before using your air fryer, thoroughly read the instruction manual. Each model may have specific care instructions and guidelines that you must follow. Familiarise yourself with the appliance's features, cleaning recommendations, and other important information provided by the manufacturer.
- **Use Non-Abrasive Utensils**: Always use non-abrasive utensils when cooking with your air fryer to avoid scratching the non-stick coating of the frying basket or other removable parts. Opt for silicone, wooden, or plastic utensils to safeguard the surfaces and steer clear of metal utensils that may damage the non-stick coating.
- **Preheat the Air Fryer:** Enhance cooking efficiency and results by preheating your air fryer before adding food. Most air fryers have a preheating function or require a few minutes of preheating time. Preheating ensures that the cooking chamber reaches the desired temperature and allows for even cooking.
- **Avoid Overcrowding:** To achieve the best cooking results, refrain from overcrowding the frying basket. Leave sufficient space between food items to enable hot air circulation. Overcrowding may lead to uneven cooking and hinder the food from becoming crispy. Cook in multiple batches if necessary.
- **Use Parchment Paper or Silicone Liners:** Prevent food from sticking to the frying basket or drip tray by using parchment paper or silicone liners. These non-stick liners make cleanup easier and protect the appliance's surfaces. Ensure that the parchment paper or silicone liner is suitable for air fryer use and can withstand high temperatures.
- **Regularly Shake or Flip the Food**: For even cooking and browning, shake or flip the food halfway through the cooking process. This ensures that all sides of the food are exposed to the circulating hot air, resulting in a crispy and evenly cooked outcome. Refer to the recipe or cooking instructions for specific shaking or flipping recommendations.
- **Cool Down Properly**: After cooking, allow your air fryer to cool down completely before cleaning or storing it. Unplug the appliance and let it sit for a while to dissipate any residual heat. This ensures your safety during the cleaning process and prevents potential damage to the appliance or other surfaces.
- **Store Properly**: When not in use, store your air fryer in a clean and dry place, free from moisture and dust. Store the removable parts separately or place them back in the air fryer if there is enough space. This helps to keep the appliance in good condition and ready for your next cooking adventure.

By following these care tips, you can maintain the quality and performance of your air fryer. Regular cleaning, proper usage, and attention to detail will ensure that your air fryer remains a reliable and versatile kitchen companion. With a well-cared-for appliance, you can continue to enjoy the benefits of healthy and delicious air-fried meals for years to come.

## Frequently Asked Questions

**Is air frying a healthier alternative to traditional frying methods?**

Compared to deep frying, air frying is generally considered a healthier cooking method. Air fryers utilise hot air circulation to cook food, requiring minimal or no oil in comparison to deep frying. This significant reduction in oil usage can greatly lower the calorie and fat content of your favourite fried foods.

## Can I use aluminium foil or other accessories in the air fryer?

Yes, you can use aluminium foil in your air fryer, but it's essential to use it correctly. Ensure that you create holes in the foil to allow hot air to circulate and promote even cooking.

Additionally, always refer to the manufacturer's instructions to determine if other accessories like baking pans or silicone moulds are safe to use with your specific air fryer model.

## How can I prevent food from sticking to the air fryer basket?

To prevent food from sticking to the air fryer basket, it's advisable to lightly coat the food with a thin layer of oil or cooking spray before placing it in the basket. Additionally, using parchment paper or silicone liners can also be helpful in preventing sticking.

## Can I cook frozen foods in an air fryer?

Yes, air fryers are excellent for cooking frozen foods. Whether it's frozen fries, chicken nuggets, or vegetables, the air fryer can cook them to crispy perfection. Simply adjust the cooking time and temperature based on the instructions provided on the food packaging or refer to air fryer cooking guides for frozen foods.

## Can I use the air fryer to reheat leftovers?

Absolutely! The air fryer is a convenient tool for reheating leftovers. It can help restore the crispiness of fried foods or provide quick and even reheating for various dishes. Just place the leftovers in the air fryer basket and heat at a moderate temperature until thoroughly heated.

## How do I clean the air fryer?

Cleaning an air fryer is typically straightforward. Begin by unplugging the appliance and allowing it to cool down. Remove the removable parts, such as the frying basket and drip tray, and wash them with warm soapy water or place them in the dishwasher if they are dishwasher-safe. Use a non-abrasive sponge or cloth to wipe down the interior and exterior of the air fryer. Always consult the manufacturer's instructions for specific cleaning guidelines.

## Can I cook different types of foods simultaneously in the air fryer?

Yes, you can cook different types of foods simultaneously in the air fryer by using dividers or racks designed for your specific model. These accessories help separate the foods, preventing flavours from mixing. However, be mindful of the cooking times and temperatures required for each food item to ensure they cook properly.

## Can I use my own recipes in an air fryer?

Absolutely! Air fryers are versatile appliances that can accommodate a wide range of recipes. You can adapt your favourite recipes by adjusting the cooking time and temperature to suit the air fryer's capabilities. Feel free to experiment with different dishes and flavours to discover new and exciting ways to use your air fryer.

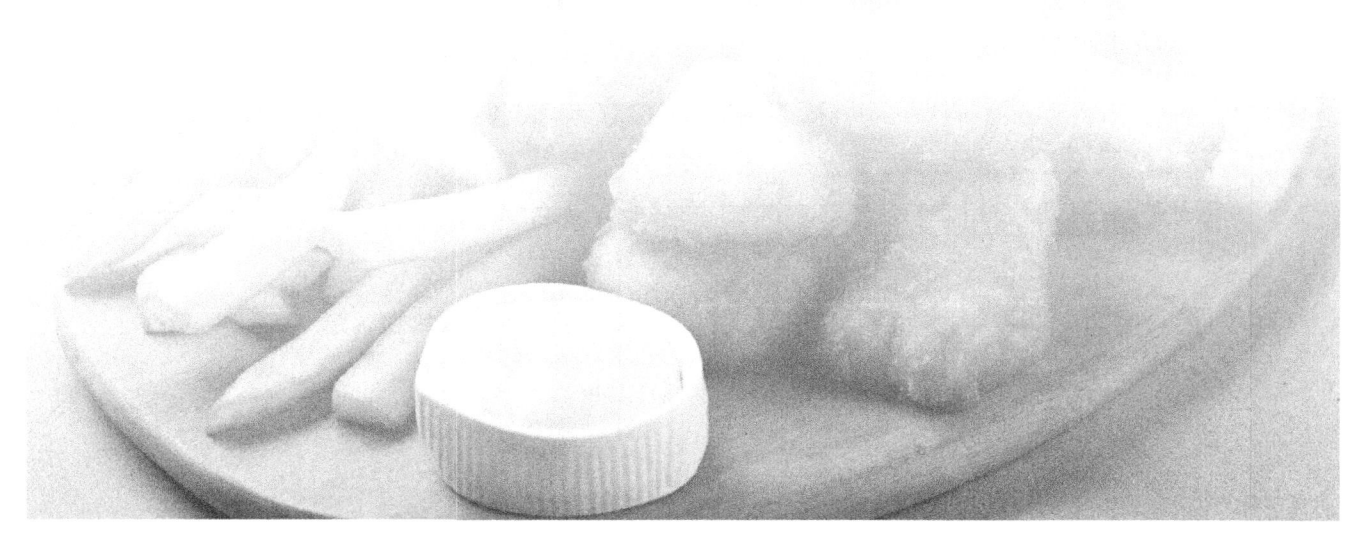

# Chapter 1: Breakfast

## Air-Fried Breakfast Tacos with Cheesy Hash Brown Shell

**Serves: 4**
**Prep time: 15 minutes / Cook time: 20 minutes**

### Ingredients:
**For the Cheesy Hash Brown Shell:**
- 200g shredded hash brown potatoes
- 50g shredded cheddar cheese
- Salt and black pepper, to taste

**For the Filling:**
- 4 cooked breakfast sausages, sliced
- 4 large eggs
- 60ml whole milk
- 1/4 tsp garlic powder
- 1/4 tsp onion powder
- Salt and black pepper, to taste
- 50g shredded cheddar cheese
- Sliced avocado, chopped tomatoes, and fresh coriander, for serving

### Preparation instructions:
1. Preheat the Air Fryer to 190°C for 5 minutes.
2. In a medium bowl, mix together the shredded hash brown potatoes, shredded cheddar cheese, salt, and black pepper.
3. Divide the hash brown mixture evenly among 4 silicone muffin cups, pressing it against the sides and bottom to form a shell.
4. Air fry the hash brown shells at 190°C for 8-10 minutes or until they are crispy and golden brown.
5. In a separate bowl, whisk together the eggs, whole milk, garlic powder, onion powder, salt, and black pepper.
6. Cook the egg mixture in a non-stick pan over medium heat, stirring gently until the eggs are softly scrambled.
7. Fill each hash brown shell with the cooked scrambled eggs, sliced breakfast sausages, and shredded cheddar cheese.
8. Return the filled tacos to the Air Fryer and air fry for another 3-5 minutes until the cheese is melted and bubbly.
9. Serve the breakfast tacos with sliced avocado, chopped tomatoes, and fresh coriander on top.

## Banana Nutella Stuffed French Toast Bites

**Serves: 4**
**Prep time: 15 minutes / Cook time: 10 minutes**

### Ingredients:
- 8 slices of white bread, crusts removed
- 2 ripe bananas, mashed
- 4 tbsp Nutella (or any chocolate hazelnut spread)
- 2 large eggs
- 60ml whole milk
- 1/2 tsp ground cinnamon
- 1/2 tsp vanilla extract
- 20g butter, melted
- Icing sugar, for dusting

### Preparation instructions:
1. In a small bowl, mix together the mashed bananas and Nutella until well combined.
2. Roll each slice of bread with a rolling pin to flatten it slightly.
3. Spread about 1 tablespoon of the banana Nutella mixture onto half of the bread slices. Top each with another slice of bread to create a sandwich.
4. Cut each sandwich into 4 equal squares to make the French toast bites.
5. In a separate bowl, whisk together the eggs, whole milk, ground cinnamon, and vanilla extract.
6. Dip each French toast bite into the egg mixture, ensuring all sides are coated.
7. Preheat the Air Fryer to 180°C for 5 minutes. Brush the Air Fryer basket with melted butter and arrange the dipped French toast bites in a single layer.
8. Air fry the French toast bites at 180°C for 5 minutes or until they are golden and crispy.
9. Dust the Banana Nutella Stuffed French Toast Bites with icing sugar before serving.

## Air-Fried Blueberry Lemon Ricotta Pancake Poppers

**Serves: 4**
**Prep time: 15 minutes / Cook time: 12 minutes**

### Ingredients:
- 120g all-purpose flour
- 1 tbsp granulated sugar
- 1 tsp baking powder
- 1/4 tsp baking soda
- 1/4 tsp salt
- 120ml buttermilk
- 1 large egg
- 60g ricotta cheese
- 1 tbsp melted butter
- 1 tsp lemon zest
- 1/2 tsp vanilla extract

- 100g fresh blueberries

**Preparation instructions:**
1. In a medium bowl, whisk together the flour, sugar, baking powder, baking soda, and salt.
2. In a separate bowl, whisk together the buttermilk, egg, ricotta cheese, melted butter, lemon zest, and vanilla extract.
3. Pour the wet Ingredients into the dry Ingredients and mix until just combined.
4. Gently fold in the fresh blueberries.
5. Preheat the Air Fryer to 180°C for 5 minutes.
6. Grease the Air Fryer basket with a little oil or cooking spray.
7. Spoon the pancake batter into the silicone muffin cups, filling each cup about two-thirds full.
8. Air fry the pancake poppers at 180°C for 10-12 minutes or until they are cooked through and lightly browned on top.
9. Let the pancake poppers cool slightly before serving. Optionally, you can dust them with icing sugar or drizzle with maple syrup.

## Sweet Potato and Bacon Breakfast Empanadas

**Serves: 4**
**Prep time: 20 minutes / Cook time: 15 minutes**

### Ingredients:
**For the Empanada Dough:**
- 200g all-purpose flour
- 1/2 tsp salt
- 100g cold unsalted butter, diced
- 1 large egg
- 2 tbsp ice water

**For the Filling:**
- 200g sweet potatoes, peeled and diced
- 100g cooked bacon, chopped
- 60g shredded cheddar cheese
- 1/4 tsp ground cumin
- 1/4 tsp paprika
- Salt and black pepper, to taste
- 1 large egg (for egg wash)

### Preparation instructions:
**For the Empanada Dough:**
1. In a food processor, pulse together the flour and salt. Add the cold diced butter and pulse until the mixture resembles coarse crumbs.
2. In a small bowl, whisk the egg with ice water, then add it to the food processor. Pulse until the dough comes together.
3. Turn the dough out onto a floured surface and knead it briefly until smooth. Wrap the dough in plastic wrap and refrigerate for at least 30 minutes.

**For the Filling and Assembly:**
1. Preheat the Air Fryer to 180°C for 5 minutes.
2. In a microwave-safe bowl, steam the diced sweet potatoes until tender. Let them cool slightly.
3. In a medium bowl, combine the cooked sweet potatoes, chopped bacon, shredded cheddar cheese, ground cumin, paprika, salt, and black pepper. Mix well.
4. Roll out the chilled empanada dough on a floured surface to about 1/8 inch thickness.
5. Cut circles from the dough using a round cutter or the rim of a glass (about 4-5 inches in diameter).
6. Spoon a tablespoon of the sweet potato and bacon filling onto one half of each dough circle.
7. Fold the other half of the dough over the filling to form a half-moon shape. Press the edges together to seal.
8. Beat the remaining egg and brush it over the tops of the empanadas for a golden finish.
9. Air fry the empanadas at 180°C for 12-15 minutes or until they are golden and crispy. Let the empanadas cool slightly before serving.

## Cinnamon Roll Apple Fritters with Cream Cheese Drizzle

**Serves: 4**
**Prep time: 20 minutes / Cook time: 10 minutes**

### Ingredients:
**For the Apple Fritters:**
- 200g all-purpose flour
- 3 tbsp granulated sugar
- 1 tsp baking powder
- 1/4 tsp salt
- 1/2 tsp ground cinnamon
- 1/4 tsp ground nutmeg
- 120ml whole milk
- 1 large egg
- 1 tsp vanilla extract
- 2 medium apples, peeled and diced
- Vegetable oil, for frying

**For the Cream Cheese Drizzle:**
- 60g cream cheese, softened
- 30ml whole milk
- 60g powdered sugar
- 1/2 tsp vanilla extract

### Preparation instructions:
**For the Cream Cheese Drizzle:**
1. In a bowl, beat the softened cream cheese until smooth.
2. Gradually add the whole milk, powdered sugar,

and vanilla extract, and mix until well combined. Set aside.

**For the Apple Fritters:**
1. In a large bowl, whisk together the flour, granulated sugar, baking powder, salt, ground cinnamon, and ground nutmeg.
2. In a separate bowl, whisk together the whole milk, egg, and vanilla extract.
3. Pour the wet Ingredients into the dry Ingredients and mix until just combined.
4. Fold in the diced apples.
5. Preheat the Air Fryer to 180°C for 5 minutes.
6. Drop spoonfuls of the apple fritter batter into the Air Fryer basket, leaving space between each fritter.
7. Air fry the apple fritters at 180°C for 8-10 minutes or until they are golden and cooked through, flipping them halfway through the cooking time for even browning.
8. Remove the apple fritters from the Air Fryer and let them cool slightly.
9. Drizzle the cream cheese mixture over the warm apple fritters before serving.

## Air-Fried Eggs in Avocado Toast Cups

**Serves: 4**
**Prep time: 10 minutes / Cook time: 6 minutes**

### Ingredients:
- 2 ripe avocados
- 4 large eggs
- Salt and black pepper, to taste
- Chopped fresh chives or parsley, for garnish

### Preparation instructions:
1. Cut the avocados in half and remove the pits.
2. Scoop out a little extra flesh from each avocado half to create a larger cavity for the egg.
3. Preheat the Air Fryer to 180°C for 5 minutes.
4. Place the avocado halves in the Air Fryer basket, so they are stable and won't tip over.
5. Crack one egg into each avocado half.
6. Season with salt and black pepper.
7. Air fry the avocado and eggs at 180°C for 5-6 minutes or until the eggs are cooked to your desired doneness.
8. Garnish with chopped fresh chives or parsley before serving.

## Breakfast Sausage and Cheese Stuffed Crescent Rolls

**Serves: 4**
**Prep time: 15 minutes / Cook time: 12 minutes**

### Ingredients:
- 1 tube (200g) refrigerated crescent roll dough
- 8 cooked breakfast sausages
- 60g shredded cheddar cheese
- 1 large egg (for egg wash)

### Preparation instructions:
1. Preheat the Air Fryer to 180°C for 5 minutes.
2. Unroll the crescent roll dough and separate the triangles.
3. Place a cooked breakfast sausage and a sprinkle of shredded cheddar cheese at the wide end of each crescent roll triangle.
4. Roll up the crescent rolls, starting from the wide end, to enclose the sausage and cheese filling.
5. Beat the egg and brush it over the tops of the stuffed crescent rolls for a golden finish.
6. Grease the Air Fryer basket with a little oil or cooking spray.
7. Arrange the stuffed crescent rolls in a single layer in the Air Fryer basket.
8. Air fry the crescent rolls at 180°C for 10-12 minutes or until they are golden brown and cooked through.
9. Let the stuffed crescent rolls cool slightly before serving.

## Lemon Poppy Seed Air-Fried Donut Holes

**Serves: 4**
**Prep time: 15 minutes / Cook time: 8 minutes**

### Ingredients:
- 120g all-purpose flour
- 2 tbsp granulated sugar
- 1 tsp baking powder
- 1/4 tsp salt
- 1/2 tsp lemon zest
- 1 tbsp poppy seeds
- 60ml whole milk
- 1 large egg
- 1 tbsp melted butter
- 1/2 tsp vanilla extract
- Vegetable oil, for frying
- 50g powdered sugar, for dusting

### Preparation instructions:
1. In a large bowl, whisk together the flour, granulated sugar, baking powder, salt, lemon zest, and poppy seeds.
2. In a separate bowl, whisk together the whole milk, egg, melted butter, and vanilla extract.
3. Pour the wet Ingredients into the dry Ingredients and mix until just combined.
4. Preheat the Air Fryer to 180°C for 5 minutes.

5. Grease the Air Fryer basket with a little oil or cooking spray.
6. Drop spoonfuls of the donut hole batter into the Air Fryer basket, leaving space between each donut hole.
7. Air fry the donut holes at 180°C for 6-8 minutes or until they are golden brown and cooked through.
8. Remove the donut holes from the Air Fryer and let them cool slightly.
9. Dust the Lemon Poppy Seed Air-Fried Donut Holes with powdered sugar before serving.

## Air-Fried Breakfast Quesadillas with Ham and Pineapple

Serves: 4
**Prep time: 15 minutes / Cook time: 8 minutes**

### Ingredients:
- 4 large flour tortillas
- 100g cooked ham, diced
- 150g shredded cheddar cheese
- 100g pineapple chunks (fresh or canned), drained
- 1/4 tsp ground cumin
- 1/4 tsp paprika
- Salt and black pepper, to taste
- Cooking spray or vegetable oil

### Preparation instructions:
1. Lay one flour tortilla on a clean surface.
2. Sprinkle diced ham, shredded cheddar cheese, and pineapple chunks evenly over half of the tortilla.
3. Season with ground cumin, paprika, salt, and black pepper.
4. Fold the other half of the tortilla over the filling to create a half-moon shape.
5. Press down gently to seal the quesadilla. Preheat the Air Fryer to 180°C for 5 minutes. Grease the Air Fryer basket with a little cooking spray or vegetable oil.
6. Place the filled quesadilla in the Air Fryer basket.
7. Air fry the breakfast quesadilla at 180°C for 4 minutes, then carefully flip it and air fry for another 4 minutes until it is crispy and the cheese is melted.
8. Remove the breakfast quesadilla from the Air Fryer and let it cool for a moment before cutting it into wedges.
9. Serve the Air-Fried Breakfast Quesadillas with Ham and Pineapple with your favorite salsa or sour cream on the side.

## Crunchy Cereal-Coated Air-Fried French Toast Sticks

Serves: 4
**Prep time: 15 minutes / Cook time: 8 minutes**

### Ingredients:
- 8 slices of white bread, crusts removed
- 60ml whole milk
- 2 large eggs
- 1/2 tsp ground cinnamon
- 1/2 tsp vanilla extract
- 100g cereal flakes (such as corn flakes or rice cereal), crushed into fine crumbs
- 30g melted butter
- Maple syrup, for serving

### Preparation instructions:
1. Preheat the Air Fryer to 180°C for 5 minutes.
2. In a shallow dish, whisk together the whole milk, eggs, ground cinnamon, and vanilla extract.
3. Cut each slice of bread into 3 long strips to make the French toast sticks.
4. Dip each bread strip into the egg mixture, coating it on all sides. In a separate dish, place the crushed cereal flakes.
5. Roll each egg-coated bread strip in the crushed cereal to coat it evenly.
6. Grease the Air Fryer basket with a little melted butter.
7. Arrange the coated French toast sticks in a single layer in the Air Fryer basket.
8. Air fry the French toast sticks at 180°C for 6-8 minutes or until they are golden and crispy.
9. Drizzle with maple syrup before serving.

## Spinach and Feta Egg Cups with Sun-Dried Tomatoes

Serves: 4
**Prep time: 15 minutes / Cook time: 12 minutes**

### Ingredients:
- 6 large eggs
- 60ml whole milk
- 50g fresh spinach, chopped
- 50g feta cheese, crumbled
- 30g sun-dried tomatoes, chopped
- 1/4 tsp dried oregano
- Salt and black pepper, to taste
- Cooking spray or vegetable oil

### Preparation instructions:
1. In a bowl, whisk together the eggs and whole milk.
2. Stir in the chopped spinach, crumbled feta cheese, chopped sun-dried tomatoes, dried oregano, salt, and black pepper.
3. Preheat the Air Fryer to 180°C for 5 minutes.
4. Grease the Air Fryer muffin cups with a little cooking spray or vegetable oil.
5. Divide the egg mixture evenly among the muffin cups.
6. Air fry the Spinach and Feta Egg Cups at 180°C

for 10-12 minutes or until the eggs are set and lightly browned on top.
7. Let the egg cups cool slightly before serving.

## Air-Fried Peanut Butter and Jelly Wontons

**Serves: 4**
**Prep time: 15 minutes / Cook time: 8 minutes**

### Ingredients:
- 12 wonton wrappers
- 60g creamy peanut butter
- 60g strawberry or grape jelly
- 1 large egg (for egg wash)
- Vegetable oil, for frying
- Icing sugar, for dusting

### Preparation instructions:
1. Lay one wonton wrapper on a clean surface.
2. Spoon a teaspoon of creamy peanut butter and a teaspoon of strawberry or grape jelly onto the centre of the wonton wrapper.
3. Brush the edges of the wonton wrapper with a little water.
4. Fold the wrapper over to create a triangle and press the edges firmly to seal the peanut butter and jelly inside.
5. Repeat with the remaining wonton wrappers and filling. Preheat the Air Fryer to 180°C for 5 minutes. Grease the Air Fryer basket with a little vegetable oil.
6. Arrange the stuffed wontons in a single layer in the Air Fryer basket.
7. Beat the egg and brush it over the tops of the wontons for a golden finish.
8. Air fry the peanut butter and jelly wontons at 180°C for 6-8 minutes or until they are golden and crispy.
9. Dust the Air-Fried Peanut Butter and Jelly Wontons with icing sugar before serving.

## Churro-Style Air-Fried Waffles with Chocolate Dipping Sauce

**Serves: 4**
**Prep time: 15 minutes / Cook time: 8 minutes**

### Ingredients:
**For the Waffles:**
- 200g all-purpose flour
- 2 tbsp granulated sugar
- 2 tsp baking powder
- 1/4 tsp salt
- 1 tsp ground cinnamon
- 250ml whole milk
- 2 large eggs
- 60ml vegetable oil

**For the Churro Coating:**
- 100g granulated sugar
- 2 tsp ground cinnamon
- 60g melted butter

**For the Chocolate Dipping Sauce:**
- 100g dark chocolate, chopped
- 60ml double cream
- 1 tbsp unsalted butter

### Preparation instructions:
1. Preheat the Air Fryer to 180°C for 5 minutes.
2. In a large bowl, whisk together the flour, sugar, baking powder, salt, and ground cinnamon.
3. In a separate bowl, whisk together the whole milk, eggs, and vegetable oil. Pour the wet Ingredients into the dry Ingredients and mix until just combined.
4. Grease the Air Fryer waffle moulds with a little cooking spray or vegetable oil.
5. Pour the waffle batter into the moulds, filling them about 2/3 full.
6. Air fry the waffles at 180°C for 6-8 minutes or until they are golden and cooked through. In a shallow dish, mix together the granulated sugar and ground cinnamon for the churro coating.
7. As soon as the waffles are done, brush them with melted butter and then roll them in the churro coating mixture until they are evenly coated.
8. For the chocolate dipping sauce, heat the double cream in a saucepan over low heat until it starts to simmer. Remove from heat and stir in the chopped dark chocolate and unsalted butter until smooth and well combined.
9. Serve the Churro-Style Air-Fried Waffles with the warm chocolate dipping sauce.

## Cheesy Spinach and Artichoke Stuffed Breakfast Mushrooms

**Serves: 4**
**Prep time: 15 minutes / Cook time: 12 minutes**

### Ingredients:
- 8 large Portobello mushrooms
- 100g baby spinach, chopped
- 100g artichoke hearts, drained and chopped
- 100g cream cheese
- 50g shredded cheddar cheese
- 1/4 tsp garlic powder
- 1/4 tsp onion powder
- Salt and black pepper, to taste
- Cooking spray or vegetable oil

### Preparation instructions:
1. Preheat the Air Fryer to 180°C for 5 minutes.
2. Remove the stems from the Portobello mushrooms

and carefully scrape out the gills to create a hollow space for the filling.
3. In a bowl, mix together the chopped baby spinach, chopped artichoke hearts, cream cheese, shredded cheddar cheese, garlic powder, onion powder, salt, and black pepper.
4. Stuff each mushroom cap with the spinach and artichoke mixture, pressing it gently to fill the cavity.
5. Grease the Air Fryer basket with a little cooking spray or vegetable oil.
6. Arrange the stuffed mushrooms in the Air Fryer basket.
7. Air fry the mushrooms at 180°C for 10-12 minutes or until the filling is heated through and the mushrooms are tender.
8. Serve the Cheesy Spinach and Artichoke Stuffed Breakfast Mushrooms warm.

## Raspberry Coconut Almond Granola Bars

**Makes: 8 bars**
**Prep time: 10 minutes / Cook time: 12 minutes**

### Ingredients:
- 120g rolled oats
- 40g shredded coconut
- 50g almonds, chopped
- 60ml coconut oil, melted
- 60ml honey
- 60g dried raspberries
- 1/2 tsp vanilla extract
- Pinch of salt

### Preparation instructions:
1. Preheat the Air Fryer to 160°C for 5 minutes.
2. In a large bowl, combine the rolled oats, shredded coconut, chopped almonds, melted coconut oil, honey, dried raspberries, vanilla extract, and a pinch of salt. Mix well to combine.
3. Line a square baking dish with parchment paper, leaving some overhang for easy removal.
4. Press the granola mixture firmly into the prepared baking dish to form an even layer.
5. Place the baking dish in the Air Fryer basket.
6. Air fry the granola bars at 160°C for 10-12 minutes or until they are lightly golden and firm.
7. Let the granola bars cool completely in the baking dish before cutting them into bars.
8. Store the Raspberry Coconut Almond Granola Bars in an airtight container.

## Air-Fried Breakfast Sushi with Banana and Nut Butter

**Serves: 4**
**Prep time: 10 minutes / Cook time: 4 minutes**

### Ingredients:
- 4 large slices of whole wheat or white bread
- 4 tbsp almond or peanut butter
- 2 large bananas, peeled and halved lengthwise
- 2 tbsp honey or maple syrup (optional)
- 1 tbsp sesame seeds (optional)

### Preparation instructions:
1. Preheat the Air Fryer to 180°C for 5 minutes.
2. Flatten each bread slice with a rolling pin to make it easier to roll.
3. Spread one tablespoon of almond or peanut butter on each bread slice.
4. Place one banana half at the edge of each bread slice and roll it up tightly, pressing the edges to seal.
5. Optionally, brush the rolled sushi with honey or maple syrup for added sweetness.
6. Grease the Air Fryer basket with a little cooking spray or vegetable oil.
7. Arrange the banana and nut butter sushi rolls in the Air Fryer basket, seam side down.
8. Air fry the breakfast sushi at 180°C for 3-4 minutes or until they are lightly toasted and crispy.
9. Optionally, sprinkle sesame seeds on top before serving.

## Greek Yoghurt and Mixed Berry Parfait Cups

**Serves: 4**
**Prep time: 10 minutes / Cook time: 5 minutes**

### Ingredients:
- 500g Greek yoghurt
- 100g mixed berries (such as strawberries, blueberries, raspberries)
- 40g honey
- 20g granola
- Fresh mint leaves, for garnish

### Preparation instructions:
1. In each serving cup or glass, layer Greek yoghurt, mixed berries, and honey.
2. Preheat the Air Fryer to 180°C for 5 minutes.
3. Repeat the layers until you reach the top of the cups.
4. Top each parfait with a sprinkle of granola for added crunch.
5. Air fry at 180°C for 5 minutes or until they are golden and crispy on the top.
6. Garnish with fresh mint leaves before serving.

## Air-Fried Quinoa and Veggie Breakfast Bites

**Serves: 4**
**Prep time: 15 minutes / Cook time: 10 minutes**

### Ingredients:

- 200g cooked quinoa
- 60g shredded cheddar cheese
- 50g finely chopped peppers (mixed colours)
- 50g finely chopped red onion
- 2 large eggs
- 1 tbsp chopped fresh parsley
- 1/4 tsp garlic powder
- 1/4 tsp onion powder
- Salt and black pepper, to taste
- Cooking spray or vegetable oil

### Preparation instructions:

1. In a large bowl, combine the cooked quinoa, shredded cheddar cheese, finely chopped peppers, finely chopped red onion, eggs, chopped fresh parsley, garlic powder, onion powder, salt, and black pepper. Mix well to combine.
2. Preheat the Air Fryer to 180°C for 5 minutes.
3. Grease the Air Fryer basket with a little cooking spray or vegetable oil.
4. Form the quinoa mixture into small bite-sized patties and place them in the Air Fryer basket.
5. Air fry the breakfast bites at 180°C for 8-10 minutes or until they are golden and crispy on the outside.
6. Serve the Air-Fried Quinoa and Veggie Breakfast Bites warm.

## Ham and Cheese Stuffed Pretzel Bites

Serves: 4
**Prep time: 20 minutes / Cook time: 12 minutes**

### Ingredients:

- 200g pizza dough (store-bought or homemade)
- 8 slices cooked ham
- 100g shredded cheddar cheese
- 1 tbsp baking soda
- 1 litre water
- Coarse sea salt, for sprinkling
- Mustard, for dipping

### Preparation instructions:

1. Preheat the Air Fryer to 180°C for 5 minutes. On a floured surface, roll out the pizza dough to about 1/4 inch thickness. Cut the rolled-out dough into small squares.
2. Place a slice of cooked ham and a sprinkle of shredded cheddar cheese in the centre of each dough square.
3. Fold the dough over the filling to create a pocket, and press the edges to seal.
4. In a large saucepan, bring the water and baking soda to a boil.
5. Drop the stuffed pretzel bites into the boiling water and blanch them for 30 seconds.
6. Remove the pretzel bites from the water with a slotted spoon and place them on a paper towel to drain excess water.
7. Grease the Air Fryer basket with a little cooking spray or vegetable oil. Arrange the stuffed pretzel bites in the Air Fryer basket.
8. Air fry the pretzel bites at 180°C for 10-12 minutes or until they are golden brown and cooked through.
9. Sprinkle the Ham and Cheese Stuffed Pretzel Bites with coarse sea salt before serving. Serve with mustard for dipping.

## Savoury Breakfast Egg Rolls with Sausage and Veggies

Serves: 4
**Prep time: 20 minutes / Cook time: 12 minutes**

### Ingredients:

- 8 egg roll wrappers
- 8 cooked breakfast sausages, thinly sliced
- 50g shredded cheddar cheese
- 50g shredded carrots
- 50g shredded cabbage
- 2 green onions, thinly sliced
- 1 tbsp soy sauce
- 1/2 tsp ground ginger
- 1/2 tsp garlic powder
- Cooking spray or vegetable oil

### Preparation instructions:

1. Preheat the Air Fryer to 180°C for 5 minutes.
2. In a bowl, mix together the sliced breakfast sausages, shredded cheddar cheese, shredded carrots, shredded cabbage, green onions, soy sauce, ground ginger, and garlic powder.
3. Place a spoonful of the sausage and vegetable filling near one corner of an egg roll wrapper.
4. Fold the corner with the filling over, tucking it tightly.
5. Fold in the side corners, and then roll the wrapper tightly to form a neat egg roll.
6. Dab a little water on the edges of the egg roll wrapper to seal it.
7. Grease the Air Fryer basket with a little cooking spray or vegetable oil. Arrange the egg rolls in the Air Fryer basket, seam side down.
8. Air fry the breakfast egg rolls at 180°C for 10-12 minutes or until they are golden and crispy.
9. Serve the Savoury Breakfast Egg Rolls with Sausage and Veggies with your favourite dipping sauce.

# Raspberry Chocolate Chip Air-Fried Muffins

- Makes: 8 muffins

**Prep time: 15 minutes / Cook time: 12 minutes**

## Ingredients:

- 200g all-purpose flour
- 100g granulated sugar
- 2 tsp baking powder
- 1/4 tsp salt
- 60ml vegetable oil
- 120ml whole milk
- 1 large egg
- 1 tsp vanilla extract
- 100g fresh raspberries
- 50g chocolate chips

## Preparation instructions:

1. Preheat the Air Fryer to 180°C for 5 minutes.
2. In a large bowl, whisk together the flour, sugar, baking powder, and salt.
3. In a separate bowl, mix together the vegetable oil, whole milk, egg, and vanilla extract.
4. Pour the wet Ingredients into the dry Ingredients and mix until just combined.
5. Gently fold in the fresh raspberries and chocolate chips.
6. Line the Air Fryer muffin cups with paper liners or grease them with a little cooking spray.
7. Divide the muffin batter evenly among the muffin cups.
8. Air fry the muffins at 180°C for 10-12 minutes or until they are golden and a toothpick inserted into the centre comes out clean.
9. Let the Raspberry Chocolate Chip Air-Fried Muffins cool slightly before serving.

# Matcha Green Tea Pancake Bites

Serves: 4
**Prep time: 15 minutes / Cook time: 8 minutes**

## Ingredients:

- 200g all-purpose flour
- 2 tbsp granulated sugar
- 1 tsp baking powder
- 1/4 tsp salt
- 1 tbsp matcha green tea powder
- 250ml whole milk
- 2 large eggs
- 1 tbsp melted butter
- 1/2 tsp vanilla extract
- Cooking spray or vegetable oil

## Preparation instructions:

1. Preheat the Air Fryer to 180°C for 5 minutes.
2. In a large bowl, whisk together the flour, sugar, baking powder, salt, and matcha green tea powder.
3. In a separate bowl, whisk together the whole milk, eggs, melted butter, and vanilla extract.
4. Pour the wet Ingredients into the dry Ingredients and mix until just combined.
5. Grease the Air Fryer pancake moulds with a little cooking spray or vegetable oil.
6. Pour the pancake batter into the moulds, filling them about 2/3 full.
7. Air fry the pancake bites at 180°C for 6-8 minutes or until they are cooked through and lightly browned on top.
8. Serve the Matcha Green Tea Pancake Bites with your favourite toppings, such as fresh fruit or maple syrup.

# Apple Cinnamon Breakfast Egg Rolls

Serves: 4
**Prep time: 20 minutes / Cook time: 10 minutes**

## Ingredients:

- 8 egg roll wrappers
- 2 large apples, peeled, cored, and thinly sliced
- 2 tbsp granulated sugar
- 1/2 tsp ground cinnamon
- 1/4 tsp ground nutmeg
- 1 tbsp lemon juice
- 1 tbsp butter, melted
- Cooking spray or vegetable oil

## Preparation instructions:

1. Preheat the Air Fryer to 180°C for 5 minutes.
2. In a bowl, toss the thinly sliced apples with granulated sugar, ground cinnamon, ground nutmeg, and lemon juice until well coated.
3. Place a spoonful of the apple mixture near one corner of an egg roll wrapper.
4. Fold the corner with the filling over, tucking it tightly.
5. Fold in the side corners, and then roll the wrapper tightly to form a neat egg roll.
6. Dab a little water on the edges of the egg roll wrapper to seal it.
7. Grease the Air Fryer basket with a little cooking spray or vegetable oil. Arrange the apple cinnamon egg rolls in the Air Fryer basket, seam side down.
8. Air fry the breakfast egg rolls at 180°C for 8-10 minutes or until they are golden and crispy.
9. Brush the Apple Cinnamon Breakfast Egg Rolls

with melted butter before serving.

Note: Adjust the sweetness according to your preference and the sweetness of the apples used.

## Air Fryer Breakfast Sausage Patties

**Serves 2-4**
**Prep time: 5 minutes / Cook time: 10-12 minutes**

### Ingredients

- 450g ground breakfast sausage
- 1/4 tsp salt
- 1/4 tsp black pepper
- 1/4 tsp garlic powder
- 1/4 tsp onion powder

### Preparation instructions

1. Preheat the air fryer to 190°C.
2. In a mixing bowl, combine the ground breakfast sausage with the salt, black pepper, garlic powder, and onion powder. Mix until well combined.
3. Form the sausage mixture into 2-3 inch patties.
4. Place the sausage patties in the air fryer basket in a single layer, making sure they are not touching.
5. Air fry for 10-12 minutes, flipping the patties halfway through, until they are browned and cooked through.
6. Remove the sausage patties from the air fryer and serve hot with your favorite breakfast sides.

## Air Fryer Banana Bread

**Serves 6**
**Prep time: 10minutes / Cook time: 30 minutes**

### Ingredients

- 2 ripe bananas, mashed
- 1/4 cup vegetable oil
- 1/2 cup granulated sugar
- 1 teaspoon vanilla extract
- 1 egg
- 1 cup all-purpose flour
- 1/2 teaspoon baking powder
- 1/2 teaspoon baking soda
- 1/2 teaspoon salt

### Preparation instructions

1. In a mixing bowl, combine the mashed bananas, vegetable oil, sugar, vanilla extract, and egg.
2. In a separate mixing bowl, whisk together the flour, baking powder, baking soda, and salt.
3. Add the dry Ingredients to the wet Ingredients and stir until just combined.
4. Pour the batter into a greased loaf pan that will fit in your air fryer basket.
5. Preheat the air fryer to 320°F (160°C).
6. Place the loaf pan in the air fryer basket and air fry for 30 minutes or until a toothpick inserted in the center comes out clean.
7. Remove from the air fryer and let cool in the pan for 10 minutes before slicing and serving.

## Air Fryer Breakfast Hash

**Serves 2**
**Prep time: 10 minutes / Cook time: 20 minutes**

### Ingredients

- 2 medium potatoes, peeled and diced
- 1/2 small onion, diced
- 1/2 small bell pepper, diced
- 2 tablespoons vegetable oil
- 1/2 teaspoon salt
- 1/4 teaspoon black pepper
- 1/4 teaspoon garlic powder
- 2 large eggs
- 2 slices bacon, cooked and crumbled

### Preparation instructions

1. Preheat the air fryer to 190°C.
2. In a large bowl, mix together the diced potatoes, onion, red pepper, green pepper, smoked paprika, garlic powder, salt, and pepper.
3. Transfer the mixture to the air fryer basket and cook for 15-20 minutes, shaking the basket occasionally to ensure even cooking.
4. Create four wells in the hash mixture and crack an egg into each well.
5. Cook for an additional 5-7 minutes or until the egg whites are set and the yolks are cooked to your desired level of doneness.
6. Serve hot and enjoy!

## Air Fryer Avocado Toast

**Serves 2**
**Prep time: 5 minutes / Cook time: 5 minutes**

### Ingredients

- 2 slices of bread
- 1 ripe avocado
- 1/4 teaspoon garlic powder
- Salt and pepper, to taste
- 2 eggs
- 1 tablespoon olive oil
- Red pepper flakes, for serving (optional)

### Preparation Instructions :

1. Preheat the air fryer to 190°C.
2. Mash the ripe avocado in a small bowl and mix in

the garlic powder, salt, and pepper.
3. Brush each slice of bread with olive oil on both sides and place them in the air fryer basket.
4. Cook for 3 minutes, flip the bread slices over, and cook for an additional 2 minutes or until they are toasted to your desired level of crispiness.
5. While the bread is toasting, crack an egg into each of the avocado halves and place them in the air fryer basket.
6. Cook for 5 minutes or until the egg whites are set and the yolks are cooked to your desired level of doneness.
7. Spread the mashed avocado on top of each toast slice and place an egg-filled avocado half on top of each.
8. Sprinkle with red pepper flakes, if desired, and serve hot.

## Cheesy Bell Pepper Eggs

**Serves 4**
**Prep time: 10 minutes / Cook time: 15 minutes**

### Ingredients
- 4 medium green peppers
- 85 g cooked ham, chopped
- ¼ medium onion, peeled and chopped
- 8 large eggs
- 235 ml mild Cheddar cheese

### Preparation instructions
1. Cut the tops off each pepper. Remove the seeds and the white membranes with a small knife. Place ham and onion into each pepper.
2. Crack 2 eggs into each pepper. Top with 60 ml cheese per pepper. Place into the air fryer basket.
3. Adjust the temperature to 200°C and air fry for 15 minutes.
4. When fully cooked, peppers will be tender and eggs will be firm. Serve immediately

## Cheddar Eggs

**Serves 2**
**Prep time: 5 minutes / Cook time: 15 minutes**

### Ingredients
- 4 large eggs
- 2 tablespoons unsalted butter, melted
- 120 ml shredded sharp Cheddar cheese

### Preparation instructions:
1. Crack eggs into a round baking dish and whisk. Place dish into the air fryer basket.
2. Adjust the temperature to 204°C and set the timer for 10 minutes.
3. After 5 minutes, stir the eggs and add the butter and cheese. Let cook 3 more minutes and stir again.
4. Allow eggs to finish cooking an additional 2 minutes or remove if they are to your desired liking.
5. Use a fork to fluff. Serve warm.

## Homemade Cherry Breakfast Tarts

**Serves: 6**
**Prep time: 15 minutes / Cook time: 20 minutes**

### Ingredients:
**Tarts:**
- 2 refrigerated piecrusts
- 80 ml cherry preServes
- 1 teaspoon cornflour
- Cooking oil

**Frosting:**
- 120 ml vanilla yoghurt
- 30 g cream cheese
- 1 teaspoon stevia
- Rainbow sprinkles

### Preparation instructions:
1. Place the piecrusts on a flat surface. Using a knife or pizza cutter, cut each piecrust into 3 rectangles, for 6 total. (I discard the unused dough left from slicing the edges.)
2. In a small bowl, combine the preServes and cornflour. Mix well.
3. Scoop 1 tablespoon of the preServes mixture onto the top half of each piece of piecrust.
4. Fold the bottom of each piece up to close the tart. Using the back of a fork, press along the edges of each tart to seal.
5. Spray the breakfast tarts with cooking oil and place them in the air fryer. I do not recommend stacking the breakfast tarts. They will stick together if stacked. You may need to prepare them in two batches. Bake at 375°F for 10 minutes.
6. Allow the breakfast tarts to cool fully before removing from the air fryer.
7. If necessary, repeat steps 5 and 6 for the remaining breakfast tarts. Make the Frosting
8. In a small bowl, combine the yoghurt, cream cheese, and stevia. Mix well.
9. Spread the breakfast tarts with frosting and top with sprinkles, and serve.

# Chapter 2: Fish and Seafood

## Crispy Coconut Shrimp with Pineapple Dipping Sauce

**Serves: 4**
**Prep time: 15 minutes / Cook time: 10 minutes**

### Ingredients:
- 400g large shrimp, peeled and deveined
- 50g all-purpose flour
- 2 large eggs, beaten
- 100g desiccated coconut
- 60ml coconut milk
- 1/2 tsp garlic powder
- 1/2 tsp onion powder
- 1/2 tsp paprika
- Salt and black pepper, to taste

### For the Pineapple Dipping Sauce:
- 100g canned crushed pineapple, drained
- 30ml mayonnaise
- 1 tbsp sweet chilli sauce
- 1 tsp lime juice
- 1/4 tsp ground ginger

### Preparation instructions:
1. Preheat the Air Fryer to 200°C for 5 minutes.
2. In a shallow dish, season the flour with garlic powder, onion powder, paprika, salt, and black pepper.
3. Dip each shrimp into the beaten eggs, then coat them in the seasoned flour.
4. Dip the flour-coated shrimp into the coconut milk, then roll them in the desiccated coconut to coat them evenly.
5. Grease the Air Fryer basket with a little cooking spray or vegetable oil.
6. Arrange the coconut-coated shrimp in the Air Fryer basket in a single layer.
7. Air fry the coconut shrimp at 200°C for 8-10 minutes or until they are golden and crispy.
8. For the pineapple dipping sauce, mix together the drained crushed pineapple, mayonnaise, sweet chilli sauce, lime juice, and ground ginger until well combined.
9. Serve the Crispy Coconut Shrimp with the Pineapple Dipping Sauce on the side.

## Cajun-Style Air-Fried Catfish Nuggets

**Serves: 4**
**Prep time: 15 minutes / Cook time: 10 minutes**

### Ingredients:
- 400g catfish fillets, cut into bite-sized nuggets
- 50g all-purpose flour
- 2 large eggs, beaten
- 100g breadcrumbs
- 1 tsp Cajun seasoning
- 1/2 tsp garlic powder
- 1/2 tsp onion powder
- Salt and black pepper, to taste

### Preparation instructions:
1. Preheat the Air Fryer to 200°C for 5 minutes.
2. In a shallow dish, mix together the breadcrumbs, Cajun seasoning, garlic powder, onion powder, salt, and black pepper.
3. Dip each catfish nugget into the beaten eggs, then coat them in the seasoned breadcrumbs.
4. Grease the Air Fryer basket with a little cooking spray or vegetable oil.
5. Arrange the coated catfish nuggets in the Air Fryer basket in a single layer.
6. Air fry the Cajun-style catfish nuggets at 200°C for 8-10 minutes or until they are golden and crispy.
7. Serve the Air-Fried Cajun-Style Catfish Nuggets with your favourite dipping sauce or tartar sauce.

## Zesty Lemon Herb Air-Fried Scallops

**Serves: 4**
**Prep time: 10 minutes / Cook time: 6 minutes**

### Ingredients:
- 400g fresh scallops, patted dry
- 60ml olive oil
- 1 lemon, juiced and zested
- 2 garlic cloves, minced
- 1 tbsp chopped fresh parsley
- 1 tbsp chopped fresh thyme
- Salt and black pepper, to taste

### Preparation instructions:
1. In a bowl, mix together the olive oil, lemon juice, lemon zest, minced garlic, chopped parsley, chopped thyme, salt, and black pepper.
2. Add the fresh scallops to the marinade and toss them to coat evenly. Let them marinate for about 5 minutes.
3. Preheat the Air Fryer to 200°C for 5 minutes.
4. Grease the Air Fryer basket with a little cooking spray or vegetable oil.
5. Arrange the marinated scallops in the Air Fryer basket in a single layer.
6. Air fry the lemon herb scallops at 200°C for 4-6 minutes or until they are opaque and cooked through.
7. Serve the Zesty Lemon Herb Air-Fried Scallops with a fresh salad or steamed vegetables.

## Spicy Sriracha Honey Glazed Air-Fried Salmon

**Serves:** 4
**Prep time:** 10 minutes / **Cook time:** 8 minutes

### Ingredients:
- 400g salmon fillets
- 60ml honey
- 2 tbsp sriracha sauce
- 1 tbsp soy sauce
- 1 tsp sesame oil
- 2 garlic cloves, minced
- 1 tbsp chopped fresh coriander
- Sesame seeds, for garnish (optional)
- Sliced green onions, for garnish (optional)

### Preparation instructions:
1. Preheat the Air Fryer to 200°C for 5 minutes.
2. In a bowl, mix together the honey, sriracha sauce, soy sauce, sesame oil, and minced garlic to make the glaze.
3. Brush the salmon fillets with the spicy sriracha honey glaze, reserving some for later.
4. Grease the Air Fryer basket with a little cooking spray or vegetable oil.
5. Arrange the glazed salmon fillets in the Air Fryer basket.
6. Air fry the spicy sriracha honey glazed salmon at 200°C for 6-8 minutes or until the salmon is cooked to your desired doneness.
7. Garnish the Air-Fried Salmon with chopped fresh coriander, sesame seeds, and sliced green onions. Serve with the remaining glaze on the side.

## Garlic Butter Parmesan Air-Fried Shrimp

**Serves:** 4
**Prep time:** 15 minutes / **Cook time:** 6 minutes

### Ingredients:
- 400g large shrimp, peeled and deveined
- 60g unsalted butter, melted
- 3 garlic cloves, minced
- 2 tbsp chopped fresh parsley
- 50g grated Parmesan cheese
- Salt and black pepper, to taste

### Preparation instructions:
1. Preheat the Air Fryer to 200°C for 5 minutes.
2. In a bowl, mix together the melted butter, minced garlic, chopped parsley, grated Parmesan cheese, salt, and black pepper.
3. Toss the peeled and deveined shrimp in the garlic butter Parmesan mixture until they are evenly coated.
4. Grease the Air Fryer basket with a little cooking spray or vegetable oil.
5. Arrange the garlic butter Parmesan shrimp in the Air Fryer basket in a single layer.
6. Air fry the shrimp at 200°C for 4-6 minutes or until they are pink and cooked through.
7. Serve the Garlic Butter Parmesan Air-Fried Shrimp with lemon wedges and a fresh salad.

## Mediterranean Herb-Stuffed Air-Fried Calamari Rings

**Serves:** 4
**Prep time:** 20 minutes / **Cook time:** 8 minutes

### Ingredients:
- 400g calamari rings
- 100g feta cheese, crumbled
- 50g black olives, pitted and chopped
- 50g sun-dried tomatoes, chopped
- 2 tbsp chopped fresh oregano
- 2 tbsp chopped fresh parsley
- 2 tbsp olive oil
- 1 lemon, juiced
- Salt and black pepper, to taste

### Preparation instructions:
1. Preheat the Air Fryer to 200°C for 5 minutes.
2. In a bowl, mix together the crumbled feta cheese, chopped black olives, chopped sun-dried tomatoes, chopped fresh oregano, chopped fresh parsley, olive oil, lemon juice, salt, and black pepper to make the stuffing.
3. Fill each calamari ring with a spoonful of the Mediterranean herb stuffing.
4. Grease the Air Fryer basket with a little cooking spray or vegetable oil.
5. Arrange the stuffed calamari rings in the Air Fryer basket in a single layer.
6. Air fry the Mediterranean herb-stuffed calamari rings at 200°C for 6-8 minutes or until they are cooked through and slightly golden.
7. Serve the Air-Fried Calamari Rings with lemon wedges and a side salad.

## Crispy Cajun Crab Cakes with Remoulade Sauce

**Serves:** 4
**Prep time:** 20 minutes / **Cook time:** 10 minutes

### Ingredients:
- 400g lump crab meat
- 60g mayonnaise
- 2 tsp Dijon mustard
- 1 tsp Cajun seasoning
- 1 tsp Worcestershire sauce

- 2 green onions, thinly sliced
- 1 red pepper, finely chopped
- 50g breadcrumbs
- 1 large egg, beaten
- Salt and black pepper, to taste

**For the Remoulade Sauce:**
- 60ml mayonnaise
- 1 tbsp Dijon mustard
- 1 tbsp chopped fresh parsley
- 1 tbsp chopped fresh chives
- 1 tbsp capers, chopped
- 1 garlic clove, minced
- 1 tsp hot sauce (optional)

**Preparation instructions:**
1. In a bowl, mix together the lump crab meat, mayonnaise, Dijon mustard, Cajun seasoning, Worcestershire sauce, thinly sliced green onions, finely chopped red bell pepper, breadcrumbs, beaten egg, salt, and black pepper to make the crab cake mixture.
2. Shape the mixture into small patties and place them on a plate.
3. Preheat the Air Fryer to 200°C for 5 minutes.
4. Grease the Air Fryer basket with a little cooking spray or vegetable oil.
5. Arrange the crab cakes in the Air Fryer basket in a single layer.
6. Air fry the Cajun crab cakes at 200°C for 8-10 minutes or until they are golden and crispy.
7. For the remoulade sauce, mix together the mayonnaise, Dijon mustard, chopped fresh parsley, chopped fresh chives, chopped capers, minced garlic, and hot sauce (if using) until well combined.
8. Serve the Crispy Cajun Crab Cakes with the Remoulade Sauce on the side.

## Crispy Coconut Lime Air-Fried Oysters

**Serves: 4**
**Prep time: 20 minutes / Cook time: 8 minutes**

**Ingredients:**
- 400g fresh oysters, shucked
- 50g all-purpose flour
- 2 large eggs, beaten
- 100g desiccated coconut
- Zest of 1 lime
- 60ml lime juice
- 1/2 tsp garlic powder
- 1/2 tsp onion powder
- Salt and black pepper, to taste

**Preparation instructions:**
1. Preheat the Air Fryer to 200°C for 5 minutes.
2. In a shallow dish, season the flour with garlic powder, onion powder, salt, and black pepper.
3. Dip each shucked oyster into the beaten eggs, then coat them in the seasoned flour.
4. Dip the flour-coated oysters into the lime juice, then roll them in the desiccated coconut to coat them evenly.
5. Grease the Air Fryer basket with a little cooking spray or vegetable oil.
6. Arrange the coconut-coated oysters in the Air Fryer basket in a single layer.
7. Air fry the coconut lime oysters at 200°C for 6-8 minutes or until they are golden and crispy.
8. Serve the Crispy Coconut Lime Air-Fried Oysters with lime wedges and a dipping sauce of your choice.

## Buffalo-Style Air-Fried Popcorn Shrimp

**Serves: 4**
**Prep time: 15 minutes / Cook time: 6 minutes**

**Ingredients:**
- 400g small shrimp, peeled and deveined
- 50g all-purpose flour
- 2 large eggs, beaten
- 100g breadcrumbs
- 1 tsp garlic powder
- 1 tsp onion powder
- 1 tsp paprika
- 60ml hot sauce
- 60 ml melted butter
- Salt and black pepper, to taste

**Preparation instructions:**
1. Preheat the Air Fryer to 200°C for 5 minutes.
2. In a shallow dish, mix together the breadcrumbs, garlic powder, onion powder, paprika, salt, and black pepper.
3. Dip each shrimp into the beaten eggs, then coat them in the seasoned breadcrumbs.
4. Grease the Air Fryer basket with a little cooking spray or vegetable oil.
5. Arrange the coated shrimp in the Air Fryer basket in a single layer.
6. Air fry the Buffalo-style popcorn shrimp at 200°C for 4-6 minutes or until they are pink and cooked through.
7. In a separate bowl, mix together the hot sauce and melted butter to make the Buffalo sauce.
8. Toss the cooked popcorn shrimp in the Buffalo sauce until they are evenly coated.
9. Serve the Buffalo-Style Air-Fried Popcorn Shrimp with celery sticks and a side of ranch or blue cheese dressing.

## Garlic and Herb Air-Fried Lobster Tails

**Serves: 4**
**Prep time: 20 minutes / Cook time: 10 minutes**

### Ingredients:
- 4 lobster tails
- 60ml olive oil
- 3 garlic cloves, minced
- 1 tbsp chopped fresh parsley
- 1 tbsp chopped fresh thyme
- 1 tbsp chopped fresh rosemary
- Salt and black pepper, to taste
- Lemon wedges, for serving

### Preparation instructions:
1. Using kitchen shears or a sharp knife, cut the top shell of each lobster tail lengthwise, exposing the meat without cutting all the way through.
2. Gently pull the meat out from the shell, leaving it attached at the base, and place it on top of the shell.
3. In a bowl, mix together the olive oil, minced garlic, chopped fresh parsley, chopped fresh thyme, chopped fresh rosemary, salt, and black pepper to make the marinade.
4. Brush the lobster tails with the garlic and herb marinade, making sure to coat the meat and the exposed part of the shell.
5. Preheat the Air Fryer to 200°C for 5 minutes.
6. Grease the Air Fryer basket with a little cooking spray or vegetable oil.
7. Arrange the marinated lobster tails in the Air Fryer basket.
8. Air fry the garlic and herb lobster tails at 200°C for 8-10 minutes or until the meat is opaque and cooked through.
9. Serve the Garlic and Herb Air-Fried Lobster Tails with lemon wedges on the side.

## Tandoori-Style Air-Fried Shrimp Tikka

**Serves: 4**
**Prep time: 15 minutes / Cook time: 6 minutes**

### Ingredients:
- 400g large shrimp, peeled and deveined
- 60ml plain yoghurt
- 1 tbsp tandoori masala spice mix
- 1 tbsp lemon juice
- 2 garlic cloves, minced
- 1 tsp grated ginger
- 1/2 tsp ground cumin
- 1/2 tsp ground coriander
- 1/4 tsp cayenne pepper (optional for extra heat)
- Salt and black pepper, to taste
- Fresh coriander leaves, for garnish

### Preparation instructions:
1. In a bowl, mix together the plain yoghurt, tandoori masala spice mix, lemon juice, minced garlic, grated ginger, ground cumin, ground coriander, cayenne pepper (if using), salt, and black pepper to make the marinade.
2. Add the peeled and deveined shrimp to the tandoori marinade and toss them to coat evenly. Let them marinate for about 10 minutes.
3. Preheat the Air Fryer to 200°C for 5 minutes.
4. Grease the Air Fryer basket with a little cooking spray or vegetable oil.
5. Arrange the marinated shrimp in the Air Fryer basket in a single layer.
6. Air fry the tandoori-style shrimp tikka at 200°C for 4-6 minutes or until they are pink and cooked through.
7. Garnish the Tandoori-Style Air-Fried Shrimp Tikka with fresh coriander leaves before serving.

## Lemon Herb Air-Fried Scampi with Linguine

**Serves: 4**
**Prep time: 20 minutes / Cook time: 10 minutes**

### Ingredients:
- 400g scampi (or large shrimp), peeled and deveined
- 200g linguine or spaghetti
- 60ml olive oil
- 1 lemon, juiced and zested
- 3 garlic cloves, minced
- 2 tbsp chopped fresh parsley
- 1 tbsp chopped fresh basil
- Salt and black pepper, to taste
- Grated Parmesan cheese, for serving

### Preparation instructions:
1. Cook the linguine or spaghetti according to the package instructions until al dente. Drain and set aside.
2. In a bowl, mix together the olive oil, lemon juice, lemon zest, minced garlic, chopped fresh parsley, chopped fresh basil, salt, and black pepper to make the lemon herb dressing.
3. Toss the peeled and deveined scampi in half of the lemon herb dressing, reserving the remaining half for later.
4. Preheat the Air Fryer to 200°C for 5 minutes.
5. Grease the Air Fryer basket with a little cooking spray or vegetable oil.
6. Arrange the lemon herb scampi in the Air Fryer

basket in a single layer.
7. Air fry the scampi at 200°C for 6-8 minutes or until they are pink and cooked through.
8. In a large bowl, toss the cooked linguine or spaghetti with the reserved lemon herb dressing until well coated.
9. Serve the Lemon Herb Air-Fried Scampi with Linguine, garnished with grated Parmesan cheese and additional chopped fresh herbs, if desired.

## Coconut Curry Air-Fried Mussels

**Serves: 4**
**Prep time: 15 minutes / Cook time: 8 minutes**

### Ingredients:
- 500g fresh mussels, cleaned and debearded
- 200ml coconut milk
- 2 tbsp red curry paste
- 1 tbsp fish sauce
- 1 tbsp brown sugar
- 1 lime, juiced
- 2 garlic cloves, minced
- 1 thumb-sized piece of ginger, grated
- 1 red chilli, sliced
- Fresh coriander leaves, for garnish

### Preparation instructions:
1. In a bowl, mix together the coconut milk, red curry paste, fish sauce, brown sugar, lime juice, minced garlic, grated ginger, and sliced red chilli to make the coconut curry sauce.
2. Place the cleaned and debearded mussels in the Air Fryer basket.
3. Pour the coconut curry sauce over the mussels, ensuring they are well coated.
4. Preheat the Air Fryer to 200°C for 5 minutes.
5. Air fry the coconut curry mussels at 200°C for 6-8 minutes or until the mussels have opened and are cooked through.
6. Garnish the Coconut Curry Air-Fried Mussels with fresh coriander leaves before serving.

## Jerk-Spiced Air-Fried Red Snapper

**Serves: 4**
**Prep time: 15 minutes / Cook time: 10 minutes**

### Ingredients:
- 4 red snapper fillets (about 150g each)
- 2 tbsp jerk seasoning
- 2 tbsp olive oil
- 1 lime, juiced
- Salt and black pepper, to taste
- Sliced scallions, for garnish
- Lime wedges, for serving

### Preparation instructions:
1. In a bowl, mix together the jerk seasoning, olive oil, lime juice, salt, and black pepper to make the jerk marinade.
2. Rub the red snapper fillets with the jerk marinade, ensuring they are well coated.
3. Preheat the Air Fryer to 200°C for 5 minutes.
4. Grease the Air Fryer basket with a little cooking spray or vegetable oil.
5. Arrange the jerk-spiced red snapper fillets in the Air Fryer basket in a single layer.
6. Air fry the red snapper at 200°C for 8-10 minutes or until they are cooked through and flake easily with a fork.
7. Garnish the Jerk-Spiced Air-Fried Red Snapper with sliced scallions and serve with lime wedges on the side.

## Almond-Crusted Air-Fried Halibut Steaks

**Serves: 4**
**Prep time: 15 minutes / Cook time: 10 minutes**

### Ingredients:
- 4 halibut steaks (about 150g each)
- 50g almond meal
- 2 tbsp grated Parmesan cheese
- 1 tsp paprika
- 1/2 tsp garlic powder
- 1/2 tsp onion powder
- 2 large eggs, beaten
- Salt and black pepper, to taste
- Lemon wedges, for serving

### Preparation instructions:
1. In a shallow dish, mix together the almond meal, grated Parmesan cheese, paprika, garlic powder, onion powder, salt, and black pepper.
2. Dip each halibut steak into the beaten eggs, then coat them in the almond mixture, pressing the mixture onto the steaks to adhere.
3. Preheat the Air Fryer to 200°C for 5 minutes.
4. Grease the Air Fryer basket with a little cooking spray or vegetable oil.
5. Arrange the almond-crusted halibut steaks in the Air Fryer basket in a single layer.
6. Air fry the halibut steaks at 200°C for 8-10 minutes or until they are cooked through and the crust is golden and crispy.
7. Serve the Almond-Crusted Air-Fried Halibut Steaks with lemon wedges on the side.

## Chipotle Lime Air-Fried Fish Tacos

**Serves: 4**
**Prep time: 20 minutes / Cook time: 8 minutes**

**Ingredients:**

- 500g white fish fillets (such as cod or tilapia)
- 2 tbsp olive oil
- 1 lime, juiced and zested
- 1 tbsp chipotle chilli powder
- 1 tsp ground cumin
- 1 tsp garlic powder
- 1/2 tsp paprika
- Salt and black pepper, to taste
- 8 small soft taco shells
- Shredded lettuce, for serving
- Diced tomatoes, for serving
- Sliced avocado, for serving
- Sour cream or yoghurt, for serving
- Fresh coriander leaves, for garnish

**Preparation instructions:**

1. In a bowl, mix together the olive oil, lime juice, lime zest, chipotle chilli powder, ground cumin, garlic powder, paprika, salt, and black pepper to make the chipotle lime marinade.
2. Rub the white fish fillets with the chipotle lime marinade, ensuring they are well coated. Let them marinate for about 10 minutes.
3. Preheat the Air Fryer to 200°C for 5 minutes.
4. Grease the Air Fryer basket with a little cooking spray or vegetable oil.
5. Arrange the chipotle lime-marinated fish fillets in the Air Fryer basket in a single layer.
6. Air fry the fish fillets at 200°C for 6-8 minutes or until they are cooked through and flake easily with a fork. Warm the taco shells according to the package instructions.
7. Assemble the Chipotle Lime Air-Fried Fish Tacos by placing a portion of the cooked fish in each taco shell.
8. Top the tacos with shredded lettuce, diced tomatoes, sliced avocado, sour cream or yoghurt, and fresh coriander leaves.
9. Serve the Chipotle Lime Air-Fried Fish Tacos immediately.

# Cajun Seafood Stuffed Eggplant Boats

**Serves: 4**
**Prep time: 20 minutes / Cook time: 20 minutes**

**Ingredients:**

- 2 large eggplants
- 300g mixed seafood (such as shrimp, crab meat, and scallops), chopped
- 1 onion, finely chopped
- 2 celery stalks, finely chopped
- 1 red pepper, finely chopped
- 3 garlic cloves, minced
- 2 tbsp Cajun seasoning
- 60ml vegetable or seafood broth
- 60ml heavy cream
- 2 tbsp chopped fresh parsley
- Salt and black pepper, to taste
- Grated Parmesan cheese, for serving

**Preparation instructions:**

1. Cut each eggplant in half lengthwise and scoop out the flesh, leaving about a 1cm thick shell. Chop the scooped-out eggplant flesh and set it aside.
2. In a large skillet, sauté the chopped onion, celery, red bell pepper, and minced garlic over medium heat until softened.
3. Add the chopped eggplant flesh and mixed seafood to the skillet, and cook for a few minutes until the seafood is cooked through.
4. Stir in the Cajun seasoning, vegetable or seafood broth, and heavy cream. Simmer for a few more minutes until the mixture thickens slightly.
5. Preheat the Air Fryer to 180°C for 5 minutes.
6. Stuff the eggplant shells with the Cajun seafood mixture.
7. Grease the Air Fryer basket with a little cooking spray or vegetable oil. Arrange the stuffed eggplant boats in the Air Fryer basket.
8. Air fry the Cajun Seafood Stuffed Eggplant Boats at 180°C for 15-20 minutes or until the eggplant shells are tender and the filling is heated through and slightly golden.
9. Garnish the stuffed eggplant boats with chopped fresh parsley and serve with grated Parmesan cheese on the side.

# Garlic and Sesame Air-Fried Soft Shell Crab

**Serves: 4**
**Prep time: 15 minutes / Cook time: 6 minutes**

**Ingredients:**

- 8 soft shell crabs
- 60ml soy sauce
- 2 tbsp sesame oil
- 2 garlic cloves, minced
- 1 thumb-sized piece of ginger, grated
- 2 tbsp sesame seeds
- 2 green onions, thinly sliced
- Lime wedges, for serving

**Preparation instructions:**

1. In a bowl, mix together the soy sauce, sesame oil, minced garlic, grated ginger, and half of the sesame seeds to make the marinade.
2. Place the soft shell crabs in the marinade and toss them to coat evenly. Let them marinate for about

10 minutes.
3. Preheat the Air Fryer to 200°C for 5 minutes.
4. Grease the Air Fryer basket with a little cooking spray or vegetable oil.
5. Arrange the marinated soft shell crabs in the Air Fryer basket in a single layer.
6. Air fry the garlic and sesame soft shell crab at 200°C for 4-6 minutes or until they are crispy and cooked through.
7. Garnish the Garlic and Sesame Air-Fried Soft Shell Crab with the remaining sesame seeds and sliced green onions.
8. Serve the soft shell crab with lime wedges on the side.

## Chimichurri Grilled Shrimp Skewers

**Serves: 4**
**Prep time: 20 minutes / Cook time: 6 minutes**

### Ingredients:
- 500g large shrimp, peeled and deveined
- 60ml olive oil
- 3 garlic cloves, minced
- 1 shallot, finely chopped
- 1 red chilli, finely chopped
- 1 tsp dried oregano
- 1/2 tsp red pepper flakes
- Salt and black pepper, to taste
- Fresh parsley leaves, for garnish

### Preparation instructions:
1. In a bowl, mix together the olive oil, minced garlic, finely chopped shallot, finely chopped red chilli, dried oregano, red pepper flakes, salt, and black pepper to make the chimichurri marinade.
2. Add the peeled and deveined shrimp to the chimichurri marinade and toss them to coat evenly. Let them marinate for about 10 minutes.
3. Preheat the Air Fryer to 200°C for 5 minutes.
4. Grease the Air Fryer basket with a little cooking spray or vegetable oil.
5. Skewer the marinated shrimp onto metal or soaked wooden skewers.
6. Arrange the shrimp skewers in the Air Fryer basket in a single layer.
7. Air fry the chimichurri grilled shrimp skewers at 200°C for 4-6 minutes or until they are pink and cooked through.
8. Garnish the Chimichurri Grilled Shrimp Skewers with fresh parsley leaves before serving.

## Crispy Cornmeal Air-Fried Catfish Po' Boys

**Serves: 4**
**Prep time: 20 minutes / Cook time: 10 minutes**

### Ingredients:
- 4 catfish fillets (about 150g each)
- 100g cornmeal
- 50g all-purpose flour
- 1 tsp paprika
- 1/2 tsp garlic powder
- 1/2 tsp onion powder
- 1/4 tsp cayenne pepper
- 2 large eggs, beaten
- 60ml buttermilk
- 4 small baguettes or sub rolls
- Shredded lettuce, for serving
- Sliced tomatoes, for serving
- Remoulade sauce, for serving (see recipe below)

**For the Remoulade Sauce:**
- 60ml mayonnaise
- 1 tbsp Dijon mustard
- 1 tbsp chopped fresh parsley
- 1 tbsp chopped fresh scallions
- 1 tbsp capers, chopped
- 1 garlic clove, minced
- 1 tsp hot sauce (optional)

### Preparation instructions:
1. In a shallow dish, mix together the cornmeal, all-purpose flour, paprika, garlic powder, onion powder, cayenne pepper, salt, and black pepper.
2. In another dish, mix together the beaten eggs and buttermilk.
3. Dip each catfish fillet into the egg-buttermilk mixture, then coat them in the cornmeal mixture, pressing the mixture onto the fillets to adhere.
4. Preheat the Air Fryer to 200°C for 5 minutes.
5. Grease the Air Fryer basket with a little cooking spray or vegetable oil.
6. Arrange the cornmeal-crusted catfish fillets in the Air Fryer basket in a single layer.
7. Air fry the catfish fillets at 200°C for 8-10 minutes or until they are crispy and cooked through.
8. Slice the baguettes or sub rolls in half lengthwise and lightly toast them. Assemble the Crispy Cornmeal Air-Fried Catfish Po' Boys by placing a catfish fillet on each roll.
9. Top the catfish with shredded lettuce, sliced tomatoes, and a generous drizzle of remoulade sauce. Serve the Crispy Cornmeal Air-Fried Catfish Po' Boys immediately.

## Caribbean-Style Air-Fried Conch Fritters

**Serves: 4**
**Prep time: 20 minutes / Cook time: 8 minutes**

**Ingredients:**

- 400g conch meat, finely chopped (substitute with shrimp if unavailable)
- 1 red pepper, finely chopped
- 1 green pepper, finely chopped
- 1 onion, finely chopped
- 2 garlic cloves, minced
- 2 tbsp chopped fresh parsley
- 2 tbsp chopped fresh thyme
- 2 tbsp chopped fresh scallions
- 2 large eggs, beaten
- 60ml milk
- 100g all-purpose flour
- 1 tsp baking powder
- 1/2 tsp cayenne pepper
- Salt and black pepper, to taste
- Vegetable oil, for greasing

**Preparation instructions:**

1. In a bowl, mix together the finely chopped conch meat (or shrimp), finely chopped red pepper, finely chopped green pepper, finely chopped onion, minced garlic, chopped fresh parsley, chopped fresh thyme, chopped fresh scallions, beaten eggs, and milk to make the fritter batter.
2. In another bowl, whisk together the all-purpose flour, baking powder, cayenne pepper, salt, and black pepper to make the dry mixture.
3. Gradually add the dry mixture to the fritter batter, stirring until well combined.
4. Preheat the Air Fryer to 200°C for 5 minutes.
5. Grease the Air Fryer basket with a little cooking spray or vegetable oil.
6. Using a spoon or scoop, drop spoonfuls of the fritter batter into the Air Fryer basket, forming small fritters.
7. Air fry the Caribbean-Style Conch Fritters at 200°C for 6-8 minutes or until they are golden and crispy on the outside and cooked through on the inside.
8. Serve the Caribbean-Style Air-Fried Conch Fritters with your favourite dipping sauce.

# Black Sesame-Crusted Air-Fried Ahi Tuna Sliders

**Serves: 4**
**Prep time: 20 minutes / Cook time: 6 minutes**

**Ingredients:**

- 400g Ahi tuna steaks
- 2 tbsp soy sauce
- 1 tbsp sesame oil
- 2 tbsp black sesame seeds
- 2 tbsp white sesame seeds
- 1 tsp grated ginger
- 1 tsp honey
- 1 tbsp lime juice
- Slider buns
- Sliced cucumber, for serving
- Wasabi mayo, for serving (see recipe below)

**For the Wasabi Mayo:**

- 60ml mayonnaise
- 1-2 tsp wasabi paste (adjust to your desired level of spiciness)
- 1 tsp soy sauce
- 1 tsp lime juice

**Preparation instructions:**

1. In a bowl, mix together the soy sauce, sesame oil, grated ginger, honey, and lime juice to make the marinade.
2. Place the Ahi tuna steaks in the marinade and toss them to coat evenly. Let them marinate for about 10 minutes. Preheat the Air Fryer to 200°C for 5 minutes.
3. In a shallow dish, mix together the black sesame seeds and white sesame seeds.
4. Remove the marinated Ahi tuna steaks from the marinade, allowing any excess marinade to drip off. Press each tuna steak into the sesame seed mixture, coating both sides.
5. Grease the Air Fryer basket with a little cooking spray or vegetable oil.
6. Arrange the sesame-crusted Ahi tuna steaks in the Air Fryer basket in a single layer.
7. Air fry the tuna sliders at 200°C for 3-4 minutes per side or until they are seared on the outside and still pink in the centre. Slice the slider buns and lightly toast them.
8. Assemble the Black Sesame-Crusted Air-Fried Ahi Tuna Sliders by placing a tuna steak on each bun.
9. Top the tuna with sliced cucumber and a dollop of wasabi mayo. Serve the sliders immediately.

**For the Wasabi Mayo:**

1. In a bowl, whisk together the mayonnaise, wasabi paste, soy sauce, and lime juice until well combined.
2. Adjust the amount of wasabi paste according to your desired level of spiciness.
3. Refrigerate the wasabi mayo until ready to use.

# Classic Fish & Chips

**Serves: 4**
**Prep time: 15 minutes / Cook time: 30 minutes**

**Ingredients:**
**For Fish**

- 4 cod fillets (250g each)
- 1 Large egg
- 80g dried breadcrumbs
- 20g grated parmesan cheese

- ¼ tsp ground pepper
- ¼ tsp sea salt
- 45g all purpose flour
- 30ml water
- Dollop of tomato ketchup (optional)

**For Chips**
- 2 Large potatoes
- 2 tbsp peanut oil
- ¼ tbsp sea salt
- ¼ tbsp ground pepper
- Vinegar

**Preparation instructions:**
1. Preheat the air fryer at 200°C for 6 minutes
2. Peel and cut the potatoes into thick chips. Using a large bowl combine all of the 'For Chips' Ingredients
3. Hand toss and fold the chips, ensuring that the potato is covered in the spices
4. Place the chips into the air fryer and select the 'air crisp' or 'air fry' function for 10-20 minutes
5. Retrieve the chips once they become golden brown in colour and crispy on the outside
6. Whilst the chips are air frying, we employ 3 more bowls. In one of the bowls, combine the flour and pepper with a fork
7. In the second bowl, beat an egg with additional water
8. In the third bowl, mix the breadcrumbs and Parmesan. Treacle sea salt onto the cod fillets
9. Coat the cod fillets with the flour mixture, then dip them into the egg mixture, followed by the breadcrumb mixture. Ensure that the cod fillets are fully covered with breadcrumb
10. Retrieve the air fried chips and toss them into an isolated warmer container or a plate, which you will cover with foil
11. Turn the air fryer back on, selecting the 'air crisp' function for 10-15 minutes
12. Once the cod becomes golden brown in appearance, remove them from the air fryer and plate them up
13. Sprinkle vinegar on top of the chips (optional), then divide the chips by 4 and place them next to the fish
14. Add a dollop of tomato ketchup on the plate as a condiment

## Fish Gratin

**Serves: 4**
**Prep time: 30 minutes / Cook time: 17 minutes**

### Ingredients:
- 1 tablespoon avocado oil
- 455 g hake fillets
- 1 teaspoon garlic powder
- Sea salt and ground white pepper, to taste
- 2 tablespoons shallots, chopped
- 1 bell pepper, seeded and chopped
- 110 g cottage cheese
- 120 ml sour cream
- 1 egg, well whisked
- 1 teaspoon yellow mustard
- 1 tablespoon lime juice
- 60 g Swiss cheese, shredded

**Preparation instructions:**
1. Brush the bottom and sides of a casserole dish with avocado oil. Add the hake fillets to the casserole dish and sprinkle with garlic powder, salt, and pepper.
2. Add the chopped shallots and bell peppers.
3. In a mixing bowl, thoroughly combine the Cottage cheese, sour cream, egg, mustard, and lime juice. Pour the mixture over fish and spread evenly.
4. Cook in the preheated air fryer at 188°C for 10 minutes.
5. Top with the Swiss cheese and cook an additional 7 minutes. Let it rest for 10 minutes before slicing and serving. Bon appétit!

## Crunchy Fish Sticks

**Serves: 4**
**Prep time: 30 minutes / Cook time: 9 minutes**

### Ingredients:
- 455 g cod fillets
- 170 g finely ground blanched almond flour
- 2 teaspoons Old Bay seasoning
- ½ teaspoon paprika
- Sea salt and freshly ground black pepper, to taste
- 60 ml mayonnaise
- 1 large egg, beaten
- Avocado oil spray
- Tartar sauce, for serving

**Preparation instructions:**
1. Cut the fish into ¾-inch-wide strips.
2. In a shallow bowl, stir together the almond flour, Old Bay seasoning, paprika, and salt and pepper to taste. In another shallow bowl, whisk together the mayonnaise and egg.
3. Dip the cod strips in the egg mixture, then the almond flour, gently pressing with your fingers to help adhere to the coating.
4. Place the coated fish on a baking paper-lined baking sheet and freeze for 30 minutes.
5. Spray the air fryer basket with oil. Set the air fryer to 204°C. Place the fish in the basket in a single layer, and spray each piece with oil.
6. Cook for 5 minutes. Flip and spray with more oil. Cook for 4 minutes more, until the internal temperature reaches 60°C. Serve with the tartar sauce.

# Chapter 3: Poultry

## Buffalo Chicken Egg Rolls with Blue Cheese Dip

Serves: 4
Prep time: 20 minutes / Cook time: 10 minutes

### Ingredients:
- 400g cooked chicken breast, shredded
- 60ml buffalo sauce
- 100g shredded mozzarella cheese
- 8 egg roll wrappers
- 1 egg, beaten (for sealing the egg rolls)
- Cooking spray or vegetable oil

**For the Blue Cheese Dip:**
- 150ml Greek yoghurt
- 50g crumbled blue cheese
- 1 tbsp chopped fresh chives
- 1 tsp lemon juice
- Salt and black pepper, to taste

### Preparation instructions:
1. In a bowl, mix together the shredded chicken, buffalo sauce, and shredded mozzarella cheese.
2. Lay an egg roll wrapper on a clean surface with one corner facing you. Place about 2 tablespoons of the buffalo chicken mixture in the centre of the wrapper.
3. Fold the bottom corner over the filling, then fold in the sides, and roll up tightly, sealing the edge with beaten egg. Repeat with the remaining wrappers and filling.
4. Preheat the Air Fryer to 200°C for 5 minutes.
5. Grease the Air Fryer basket with a little cooking spray or vegetable oil.
6. Arrange the buffalo chicken egg rolls in the Air Fryer basket in a single layer.
7. Air fry the egg rolls at 200°C for 8-10 minutes or until they are golden and crispy.
8. For the blue cheese dip, mix together the Greek yoghurt, crumbled blue cheese, chopped fresh chives, lemon juice, salt, and black pepper in a small bowl.
9. Serve the Buffalo Chicken Egg Rolls with the Blue Cheese Dip.

## Chimichurri Lime Air-Fried Chicken Thighs

Serves: 4
Prep time: 15 minutes / Cook time: 20 minutes

### Ingredients:
- 8 chicken thighs, bone-in and skin-on
- 60ml olive oil
- 2 limes, juiced and zested
- 3 garlic cloves, minced
- 2 tbsp chopped fresh parsley
- 2 tbsp chopped fresh coriander
- 1 tbsp chopped fresh oregano
- Salt and black pepper, to taste

### Preparation instructions:
1. In a bowl, mix together the olive oil, lime juice, lime zest, minced garlic, chopped fresh parsley, chopped fresh coriander, chopped fresh oregano, salt, and black pepper to make the chimichurri marinade.
2. Add the chicken thighs to the marinade and toss them to coat evenly. Let them marinate for at least 30 minutes, or preferably, overnight in the refrigerator.
3. Preheat the Air Fryer to 200°C for 5 minutes.
4. Grease the Air Fryer basket with a little cooking spray or vegetable oil.
5. Arrange the marinated chicken thighs in the Air Fryer basket in a single layer.
6. Air fry the chicken thighs at 200°C for 18-20 minutes or until they are cooked through and the skin is crispy.
7. Serve the Chimichurri Lime Air-Fried Chicken Thighs with your favourite side dishes.

## Korean BBQ Air-Fried Chicken Wings

Serves: 4
Prep time: 10 minutes / Cook time: 20 minutes

### Ingredients:
- 1kg chicken wings
- 60ml soy sauce
- 2 tbsp gochujang (Korean red pepper paste)
- 2 tbsp honey
- 2 garlic cloves, minced
- 1 thumb-sized piece of ginger, grated
- 1 tbsp sesame oil
- 1 tbsp sesame seeds
- 2 green onions, thinly sliced
- Lime wedges, for serving

### Preparation instructions:
1. In a bowl, mix together the soy sauce, gochujang, honey, minced garlic, grated ginger, and sesame oil to make the Korean BBQ marinade.
2. Add the chicken wings to the marinade and toss

them to coat evenly. Let them marinate for at least 30 minutes, or preferably, overnight in the refrigerator.
3. Preheat the Air Fryer to 200°C for 5 minutes.
4. Grease the Air Fryer basket with a little cooking spray or vegetable oil.
5. Arrange the marinated chicken wings in the Air Fryer basket in a single layer.
6. Air fry the chicken wings at 200°C for 18-20 minutes or until they are cooked through and crispy.
7. Sprinkle the Korean BBQ Air-Fried Chicken Wings with sesame seeds and sliced green onions.
8. Serve the chicken wings with lime wedges on the side.

## Stuffed Pesto and Mozzarella Air-Fried Chicken Breasts

**Serves: 4**
**Prep time: 20 minutes / Cook time: 20 minutes**

### Ingredients:
- 4 chicken breasts
- 60ml pesto sauce
- 100g fresh mozzarella cheese, sliced
- 100g cherry tomatoes, halved
- 1 tbsp olive oil
- Salt and black pepper, to taste
- Fresh basil leaves, for garnish

### Preparation instructions:
1. Make a pocket in each chicken breast by cutting a slit horizontally through the thickest part, without cutting all the way through.
2. Spread pesto sauce inside each pocket, then stuff each chicken breast with sliced mozzarella and halved cherry tomatoes.
3. Preheat the Air Fryer to 200°C for 5 minutes.
4. Grease the Air Fryer basket with a little cooking spray or vegetable oil.
5. Brush the stuffed chicken breasts with olive oil and season with salt and black pepper.
6. Arrange the stuffed chicken breasts in the Air Fryer basket in a single layer.
7. Air fry the chicken breasts at 200°C for 18-20 minutes or until they are cooked through and the cheese is melted and bubbly.
8. Garnish the Stuffed Pesto and Mozzarella Air-Fried Chicken Breasts with fresh basil leaves before serving.

## Coconut Curry Air-Fried Chicken Skewers

**Serves: 4**
**Prep time: 20 minutes / Cook time: 10 minutes**

### Ingredients:
- 500g chicken breast, cut into bite-sized pieces
- 200ml coconut milk
- 2 tbsp red curry paste
- 1 tbsp fish sauce
- 1 tbsp brown sugar
- 1 lime, juiced
- 2 garlic cloves, minced
- 1 thumb-sized piece of ginger, grated
- Salt and black pepper, to taste
- Wooden skewers, soaked in water for 30 minutes
- Fresh coriander leaves, for garnish

### Preparation instructions:
1. In a bowl, mix together the coconut milk, red curry paste, fish sauce, brown sugar, lime juice, minced garlic, grated ginger, salt, and black pepper to make the coconut curry marinade.
2. Add the chicken pieces to the coconut curry marinade and toss them to coat evenly. Let them marinate for about 30 minutes.
3. Preheat the Air Fryer to 200°C for 5 minutes.
4. Thread the marinated chicken pieces onto the soaked wooden skewers.
5. Grease the Air Fryer basket with a little cooking spray or vegetable oil.
6. Arrange the chicken skewers in the Air Fryer basket in a single layer.
7. Air fry the chicken skewers at 200°C for 8-10 minutes or until they are cooked through and slightly charred.
8. Garnish the Coconut Curry Air-Fried Chicken Skewers with fresh coriander leaves before serving.

## Honey Mustard Pretzel-Crusted Air-Fried Chicken Bites

**Serves: 4**
**Prep time: 20 minutes / Cook time: 10 minutes**

### Ingredients:
- 500g boneless, skinless chicken breasts, cut into bite-sized pieces
- 60ml Dijon mustard
- 60ml honey
- 1 tbsp apple cider vinegar
- 100g pretzel crumbs (made by crushing pretzels in a food processor)
- Salt and black pepper, to taste
- Cooking spray or vegetable oil

### Preparation instructions:
1. In a bowl, mix together the Dijon mustard, honey, apple cider vinegar, salt, and black pepper to make the honey mustard marinade.
2. Add the chicken pieces to the honey mustard

marinade and toss them to coat evenly. Let them marinate for about 10 minutes.
3. Preheat the Air Fryer to 200°C for 5 minutes. In a separate shallow dish, place the pretzel crumbs.
4. Remove the marinated chicken pieces from the marinade, allowing any excess marinade to drip off.
5. Coat each chicken piece with pretzel crumbs, pressing the crumbs onto the chicken to adhere.
6. Grease the Air Fryer basket with a little cooking spray or vegetable oil.
7. Arrange the pretzel-crusted chicken bites in the Air Fryer basket in a single layer.
8. Air fry the chicken bites at 200°C for 8-10 minutes or until they are cooked through and crispy.
9. Serve the Honey Mustard Pretzel-Crusted Air-Fried Chicken Bites with your favourite dipping sauce.

## Jerk-Spiced Air-Fried Turkey Meatballs

**Serves: 4**
**Prep time: 20 minutes / Cook time: 10 minutes**

### Ingredients:
- 500g minced turkey
- 1 egg, beaten
- 60ml breadcrumbs
- 2 green onions, finely chopped
- 1 garlic clove, minced
- 1 thumb-sized piece of ginger, grated
- 2 tbsp jerk seasoning
- Salt and black pepper, to taste
- Cooking spray or vegetable oil

### Preparation instructions:
1. In a bowl, mix together the minced turkey, beaten egg, breadcrumbs, finely chopped green onions, minced garlic, grated ginger, jerk seasoning, salt, and black pepper to make the jerk-spiced meatball mixture.
2. Shape the mixture into small meatballs, about 3cm in diameter.
3. Preheat the Air Fryer to 200°C for 5 minutes.
4. Grease the Air Fryer basket with a little cooking spray or vegetable oil.
5. Arrange the turkey meatballs in the Air Fryer basket in a single layer.
6. Air fry the jerk-spiced turkey meatballs at 200°C for 8-10 minutes or until they are cooked through and slightly browned.
7. Serve the Jerk-Spiced Air-Fried Turkey Meatballs with your favourite side dishes.

## Garlic Herb Butter Air-Fried Cornish Hens

**Serves: 4**
**Prep time: 15 minutes / Cook time: 40 minutes**

### Ingredients:
- 2 Cornish hens (about 500g each)
- 60g unsalted butter, softened
- 2 garlic cloves, minced
- 1 tbsp chopped fresh parsley
- 1 tbsp chopped fresh thyme
- 1 tbsp chopped fresh rosemary
- Salt and black pepper, to taste
- Cooking spray or vegetable oil

### Preparation instructions:
1. In a bowl, mix together the softened unsalted butter, minced garlic, chopped fresh parsley, chopped fresh thyme, chopped fresh rosemary, salt, and black pepper to make the garlic herb butter.
2. Preheat the Air Fryer to 200°C for 5 minutes. Pat the Cornish hens dry with paper towels.
3. Carefully loosen the skin of the hens by sliding your fingers under the skin, being careful not to tear it.
4. Rub the garlic herb butter under the skin and all over the hens, coating them evenly.
5. Grease the Air Fryer basket with a little cooking spray or vegetable oil.
6. Place the Cornish hens in the Air Fryer basket, breast side down.
7. Air fry the garlic herb butter Cornish hens at 200°C for 20 minutes.
8. Carefully flip the hens and air fry for an additional 15-20 minutes or until they are cooked through and the skin is golden and crispy.
9. Serve the Garlic Herb Butter Air-Fried Cornish Hens with your favourite side dishes.

## Greek Yoghurt and Herb Marinated Air-Fried Turkey Cutlets

**Serves: 4**
**Prep time: 20 minutes / Cook time: 10 minutes**

### Ingredients:
- 500g turkey cutlets
- 150g Greek yoghurt
- 2 garlic cloves, minced
- 1 lemon, juiced and zested
- 2 tbsp chopped fresh oregano
- 2 tbsp chopped fresh thyme
- Salt and black pepper, to taste
- Cooking spray or vegetable oil

### Preparation instructions:
1. In a bowl, mix together the Greek yoghurt, minced garlic, lemon juice, lemon zest, chopped fresh oregano, chopped fresh thyme, salt, and black pepper to make the marinade.

2. Add the turkey cutlets to the marinade and toss them to coat evenly. Let them marinate for at least 30 minutes, or preferably, overnight in the refrigerator.
3. Preheat the Air Fryer to 200°C for 5 minutes.
4. Grease the Air Fryer basket with a little cooking spray or vegetable oil.
5. Arrange the marinated turkey cutlets in the Air Fryer basket in a single layer.
6. Air fry the turkey cutlets at 200°C for 8-10 minutes or until they are cooked through and slightly browned.
7. Serve the Greek Yoghurt and Herb Marinated Air-Fried Turkey Cutlets with your favourite side dishes.

## Maple Sriracha Glazed Air-Fried Duck Breast

**Serves: 4**
**Prep time: 15 minutes / Cook time: 20 minutes**

### Ingredients:
- 4 duck breasts
- 60ml maple syrup
- 2 tbsp soy sauce
- 2 tbsp sriracha sauce
- 2 garlic cloves, minced
- 1 thumb-sized piece of ginger, grated
- Salt and black pepper, to taste
- Cooking spray or vegetable oil

### Preparation instructions:
1. In a bowl, mix together the maple syrup, soy sauce, sriracha sauce, minced garlic, grated ginger, salt, and black pepper to make the glaze.
2. Score the skin of the duck breasts with a sharp knife in a crisscross pattern.
3. Brush the duck breasts with the glaze, coating them evenly.
4. Preheat the Air Fryer to 200°C for 5 minutes.
5. Grease the Air Fryer basket with a little cooking spray or vegetable oil.
6. Arrange the glazed duck breasts in the Air Fryer basket, skin side up.
7. Air fry the duck breasts at 200°C for 18-20 minutes or until they are cooked to your desired level of doneness.
8. Let the duck breasts rest for a few minutes before slicing and serving.
9. Serve the Maple Sriracha Glazed Air-Fried Duck Breast with your favourite side dishes.

## Panko-Crusted Air-Fried Chicken Cordon Bleu

**Serves: 4**
**Prep time: 20 minutes / Cook time: 15 minutes**

### Ingredients:
- 4 chicken breasts, boneless and skinless
- 100g Swiss cheese, sliced
- 100g cooked ham, sliced
- 2 large eggs, beaten
- 60ml milk
- 100g panko breadcrumbs
- 1/2 tsp garlic powder
- 1/2 tsp onion powder
- Salt and black pepper, to taste
- Cooking spray or vegetable oil

### Preparation instructions:
1. Preheat the Air Fryer to 200°C for 5 minutes.
2. Make a pocket in each chicken breast by cutting a slit horizontally through the thickest part, without cutting all the way through.
3. Stuff each chicken breast with slices of Swiss cheese and cooked ham.
4. In a shallow dish, whisk together the beaten eggs and milk.
5. In another shallow dish, mix together the panko breadcrumbs, garlic powder, onion powder, salt, and black pepper. Dip each stuffed chicken breast into the egg mixture, allowing any excess to drip off.
6. Coat the chicken breasts with the panko breadcrumb mixture, pressing the breadcrumbs onto the chicken to adhere. Grease the Air Fryer basket with a little cooking spray or vegetable oil.
7. Arrange the panko-crusted chicken cordon bleu in the Air Fryer basket in a single layer.
8. Air fry the chicken cordon bleu at 200°C for 12-15 minutes or until they are cooked through and the breadcrumbs are golden and crispy.
9. Serve the Panko-Crusted Air-Fried Chicken Cordon Bleu with your favourite side dishes.

## Ranch and Bacon Air-Fried Chicken Sliders

**Serves: 4**
**Prep time: 20 minutes / Cook time: 15 minutes**

### Ingredients:
- 500g ground chicken
- 60ml ranch dressing
- 4 slices cooked bacon, crumbled
- 50g breadcrumbs
- 1 large egg, beaten
- 1 tsp dried parsley
- 1/2 tsp garlic powder
- 1/2 tsp onion powder
- Salt and black pepper, to taste
- Slider buns
- Lettuce, tomato slices, and red onion slices, for serving

**Preparation instructions:**

1. In a bowl, mix together the ground chicken, ranch dressing, crumbled bacon, breadcrumbs, beaten egg, dried parsley, garlic powder, onion powder, salt, and black pepper to make the chicken slider mixture.
2. Shape the mixture into small slider-sized patties.
3. Preheat the Air Fryer to 200°C for 5 minutes.
4. Grease the Air Fryer basket with a little cooking spray or vegetable oil.
5. Arrange the chicken sliders in the Air Fryer basket in a single layer.
6. Air fry the chicken sliders at 200°C for 12-15 minutes or until they are cooked through and slightly browned.
7. Serve the Ranch and Bacon Air-Fried Chicken Sliders on slider buns with lettuce, tomato slices, and red onion slices.

## Hawaiian Pineapple Teriyaki Air-Fried Chicken Skewers

**Serves: 4**
**Prep time: 30 minutes / Cook time: 10 minutes**

**Ingredients:**

- 500g chicken breast, cut into bite-sized pieces
- 200g pineapple chunks
- 60ml teriyaki sauce
- 2 tbsp soy sauce
- 2 tbsp honey
- 1 tbsp rice vinegar
- 1 tsp grated ginger
- 1 garlic clove, minced
- Salt and black pepper, to taste
- Wooden skewers, soaked in water for 30 minutes
- Sesame seeds and chopped green onions, for garnish

**Preparation instructions:**

1. In a bowl, mix together the teriyaki sauce, soy sauce, honey, rice vinegar, grated ginger, minced garlic, salt, and black pepper to make the teriyaki marinade.
2. Add the chicken pieces to the teriyaki marinade and toss them to coat evenly. Let them marinate for about 20 minutes.
3. Preheat the Air Fryer to 200°C for 5 minutes.
4. Thread the marinated chicken pieces and pineapple chunks onto the soaked wooden skewers.
5. Grease the Air Fryer basket with a little cooking spray or vegetable oil.
6. Arrange the chicken skewers in the Air Fryer basket in a single layer.
7. Air fry the chicken skewers at 200°C for 8-10 minutes or until the chicken is cooked through and slightly charred.
8. Garnish the Hawaiian Pineapple Teriyaki Air-Fried Chicken Skewers with sesame seeds and chopped green onions before serving.

## Lemon Dill Air-Fried Chicken Schnitzel

**Serves: 4**
**Prep time: 20 minutes / Cook time: 12 minutes**

**Ingredients:**

- 4 chicken breasts, boneless and skinless
- 100g all-purpose flour
- 2 large eggs, beaten
- 60ml milk
- 150g breadcrumbs
- 1 tbsp chopped fresh dill
- Zest of 1 lemon
- 1/2 tsp garlic powder
- 1/2 tsp onion powder
- Salt and black pepper, to taste
- Cooking spray or vegetable oil

**Preparation instructions:**

1. Preheat the Air Fryer to 200°C for 5 minutes. Place each chicken breast between two pieces of plastic wrap and pound them with a meat mallet until they are about 1 cm thick.
2. In a shallow dish, place the all-purpose flour. In another shallow dish, whisk together the beaten eggs and milk.
3. In a third shallow dish, mix together the breadcrumbs, chopped fresh dill, lemon zest, garlic powder, onion powder, salt, and black pepper to make the breadcrumb mixture.
4. Dredge each chicken schnitzel in the flour, shaking off any excess.
5. Dip the chicken schnitzels into the egg mixture, allowing any excess to drip off.
6. Coat the chicken schnitzels with the breadcrumb mixture, pressing the breadcrumbs onto the chicken to adhere.
7. Grease the Air Fryer basket with a little cooking spray or vegetable oil. Arrange the lemon dill chicken schnitzels in the Air Fryer basket in a single layer.
8. Air fry the chicken schnitzels at 200°C for 10-12 minutes or until they are cooked through and the breadcrumbs are golden and crispy.
9. Serve the Lemon Dill Air-Fried Chicken Schnitzel with lemon wedges and your favourite side dishes.

## Spinach and Feta Stuffed Air-Fried Chicken Rolls

**Serves: 4**
**Prep time: 25 minutes / Cook time: 15 minutes**

### Ingredients:
- 4 chicken breasts, boneless and skinless
- 100g baby spinach, blanched and chopped
- 100g feta cheese, crumbled
- 2 garlic cloves, minced
- 1 tsp dried oregano
- 1/2 tsp dried thyme
- Salt and black pepper, to taste
- Cooking spray or vegetable oil

### Preparation instructions:
1. Preheat the Air Fryer to 200°C for 5 minutes.
2. Make a pocket in each chicken breast by cutting a slit horizontally through the thickest part, without cutting all the way through.
3. In a bowl, mix together the chopped baby spinach, crumbled feta cheese, minced garlic, dried oregano, dried thyme, salt, and black pepper to make the spinach and feta stuffing.
4. Stuff each chicken breast with the spinach and feta mixture.
5. Grease the Air Fryer basket with a little cooking spray or vegetable oil.
6. Arrange the stuffed chicken rolls in the Air Fryer basket in a single layer.
7. Air fry the chicken rolls at 200°C for 12-15 minutes or until they are cooked through and slightly browned.
8. Serve the Spinach and Feta Stuffed Air-Fried Chicken Rolls with your favourite side dishes.

## Cajun Sweet Potato Air-Fried Chicken Bites

**Serves: 4**
**Prep time: 20 minutes / Cook time: 12 minutes**

### Ingredients:
- 500g chicken breast, cut into bite-sized pieces
- 1 large sweet potato, peeled and cut into small cubes
- 60ml buttermilk
- 60g all-purpose flour
- 1 tbsp Cajun seasoning
- 1/2 tsp garlic powder
- 1/2 tsp onion powder
- Salt and black pepper, to taste
- Cooking spray or vegetable oil

### Preparation instructions:
1. Preheat the Air Fryer to 200°C for 5 minutes.
2. In a bowl, mix together the buttermilk, Cajun seasoning, garlic powder, onion powder, salt, and black pepper to make the marinade.
3. Add the chicken pieces to the marinade and toss them to coat evenly. Let them marinate for about 10 minutes.
4. In a separate bowl, toss the sweet potato cubes with all-purpose flour, ensuring they are coated evenly.
5. Grease the Air Fryer basket with a little cooking spray or vegetable oil.
6. Arrange the marinated chicken pieces and coated sweet potato cubes in the Air Fryer basket in a single layer.
7. Air fry the Cajun sweet potato chicken bites at 200°C for 10-12 minutes or until the chicken is cooked through and the sweet potatoes are tender and slightly crispy.
8. Serve the Cajun Sweet Potato Air-Fried Chicken Bites with your favourite dipping sauce.

## BBQ Pulled Chicken Air-Fried Sweet Potato Skins

**Serves: 4**
**Prep time: 30 minutes / Cook time: 15 minutes**

### Ingredients:
- 2 large sweet potatoes
- 300g cooked chicken, shredded
- 60ml barbecue sauce
- 1/2 red onion, finely diced
- 60g shredded cheddar cheese
- 2 green onions, thinly sliced
- Cooking spray or vegetable oil

### Preparation instructions:
1. Preheat the Air Fryer to 200°C for 5 minutes.
2. Wash and scrub the sweet potatoes, then pat them dry with paper towels. Pierce the sweet potatoes with a fork several times to allow steam to escape during cooking.
3. Place the sweet potatoes in the Air Fryer basket. Air fry the sweet potatoes at 200°C for 25-30 minutes or until they are tender.
4. Let the sweet potatoes cool slightly, then cut them in half lengthwise. Scoop out the flesh, leaving about a 1/4-inch thick layer of sweet potato inside the skin.
5. In a bowl, mix together the shredded chicken and barbecue sauce to make the pulled chicken filling.
6. Grease the Air Fryer basket with a little cooking spray or vegetable oil. Stuff each sweet potato skin with the pulled chicken filling.
7. Arrange the stuffed sweet potato skins in the Air Fryer basket in a single layer.
8. Air fry the BBQ Pulled Chicken Air-Fried Sweet Potato Skins at 200°C for 10-15 minutes or until the filling is heated through and the edges of the sweet potato skins are crispy.
9. Garnish the sweet potato skins with diced red onion, shredded cheddar cheese, and sliced green onions before serving.

# Mediterranean Herb Air-Fried Quail with Olives and Feta

**Serves: 4**
**Prep time: 30 minutes / Cook time: 15 minutes**

## Ingredients:
- 8 quails
- 60ml olive oil
- 2 garlic cloves, minced
- 1 tbsp chopped fresh thyme
- 1 tbsp chopped fresh rosemary
- 1 tbsp chopped fresh oregano
- Salt and black pepper, to taste
- 100g Kalamata olives, pitted and halved
- 100g feta cheese, crumbled
- Cooking spray or vegetable oil

## Preparation instructions:
1. In a bowl, mix together the olive oil, minced garlic, chopped fresh thyme, chopped fresh rosemary, chopped fresh oregano, salt, and black pepper to make the herb marinade.
2. Add the quails to the herb marinade and toss them to coat evenly. Let them marinate for about 20 minutes.
3. Preheat the Air Fryer to 200°C for 5 minutes.
4. Grease the Air Fryer basket with a little cooking spray or vegetable oil.
5. Arrange the marinated quails in the Air Fryer basket in a single layer.
6. Air fry the Mediterranean herb quails at 200°C for 10-15 minutes or until they are cooked through and slightly browned.
7. Serve the Air-Fried Quail with Olives and Feta with your favourite side dishes.

# Thai Red Curry Air-Fried Chicken Lettuce Wraps

**Serves: 4**
**Prep time: 30 minutes / Cook time: 10 minutes**

## Ingredients:
- 500g chicken breast, minced
- 60ml Thai red curry paste
- 2 tbsp fish sauce
- 1 tbsp soy sauce
- 2 tsp brown sugar
- 1 red pepper, finely diced
- 1 carrot, grated
- 4-6 large lettuce leaves (such as butter or iceberg lettuce)
- Chopped fresh coriander and chopped peanuts, for garnish
- Cooking spray or vegetable oil

## Preparation instructions:
1. Preheat the Air Fryer to 200°C for 5 minutes.
2. In a bowl, mix together the Thai red curry paste, fish sauce, soy sauce, and brown sugar to make the red curry marinade.
3. Add the minced chicken to the red curry marinade and toss it to coat evenly. Let it marinate for about 20 minutes.
4. Grease the Air Fryer basket with a little cooking spray or vegetable oil.
5. Arrange the marinated minced chicken in the Air Fryer basket in a single layer.
6. Air fry the Thai red curry chicken at 200°C for 8-10 minutes or until it is cooked through and slightly browned.
7. In a separate bowl, mix together the finely diced red pepper and grated carrot to make the vegetable filling.
8. To serve, spoon the cooked red curry chicken into lettuce leaves and top with the vegetable filling.
9. Garnish the Thai Red Curry Air-Fried Chicken Lettuce Wraps with chopped fresh coriander and chopped peanuts.

# Rosemary and Garlic Air-Fried Chicken Legs

**Serves: 4**
**Prep time: 20 minutes / Cook time: 25 minutes**

## Ingredients:
- 8 chicken drumsticks
- 60ml olive oil
- 4 garlic cloves, minced
- 2 tbsp chopped fresh rosemary
- Zest of 1 lemon
- Salt and black pepper, to taste
- Cooking spray or vegetable oil

## Preparation instructions:
1. Preheat the Air Fryer to 200°C for 5 minutes.
2. In a bowl, mix together the olive oil, minced garlic, chopped fresh rosemary, lemon zest, salt, and black pepper to make the rosemary and garlic marinade.
3. Add the chicken drumsticks to the rosemary and garlic marinade and toss them to coat evenly. Let them marinate for about 15 minutes.
4. Grease the Air Fryer basket with a little cooking spray or vegetable oil.
5. Arrange the marinated chicken drumsticks in the Air Fryer basket in a single layer.
6. Air fry the rosemary and garlic chicken legs at 200°C for 20-25 minutes or until they are cooked through and the skin is crispy.
7. Serve the Rosemary and Garlic Air-Fried Chicken Legs with your favourite side dishes.

# Cranberry and Brie Stuffed Air-Fried Chicken Breasts

**Serves: 4**
**Prep time: 30 minutes / Cook time: 15 minutes**

## Ingredients:

- 4 chicken breasts, boneless and skinless
- 100g Brie cheese, sliced
- 100g dried cranberries
- 2 tbsp chopped fresh sage
- 2 tbsp chopped fresh thyme
- Salt and black pepper, to taste
- Cooking spray or vegetable oil

## Preparation instructions:

1. Preheat the Air Fryer to 200°C for 5 minutes.
2. Make a pocket in each chicken breast by cutting a slit horizontally through the thickest part, without cutting all the way through.
3. Stuff each chicken breast with slices of Brie cheese and dried cranberries.
4. In a bowl, mix together the chopped fresh sage, chopped fresh thyme, salt, and black pepper to make the herb seasoning.
5. Season the stuffed chicken breasts with the herb seasoning, rubbing it on the outside of the chicken.
6. Grease the Air Fryer basket with a little cooking spray or vegetable oil.
7. Arrange the stuffed chicken breasts in the Air Fryer basket in a single layer.
8. Air fry the cranberry and Brie stuffed chicken breasts at 200°C for 12-15 minutes or until they are cooked through and slightly browned.
9. Serve the Cranberry and Brie Stuffed Air-Fried Chicken Breasts with your favourite side dishes.

# Spicy Honey Lime Air-Fried Chicken Wings

**Serves: 4**
**Prep time: 30 minutes / Cook time: 25 minutes**

## Ingredients:

- 1kg chicken wings
- 60ml honey
- 2 tbsp lime juice
- 1 tbsp soy sauce
- 1 tbsp sriracha sauce
- 1 tsp garlic powder
- 1 tsp onion powder
- 1/2 tsp cayenne pepper (adjust to your desired level of spiciness)
- Salt and black pepper, to taste
- Cooking spray or vegetable oil

## Preparation instructions:

1. Preheat the Air Fryer to 200°C for 5 minutes.
2. In a bowl, mix together the honey, lime juice, soy sauce, sriracha sauce, garlic powder, onion powder, cayenne pepper, salt, and black pepper to make the spicy honey lime glaze.
3. In a separate bowl, toss the chicken wings with half of the spicy honey lime glaze, ensuring they are coated evenly.
4. Grease the Air Fryer basket with a little cooking spray or vegetable oil.
5. Arrange the glazed chicken wings in the Air Fryer basket in a single layer.
6. Air fry the chicken wings at 200°C for 20-25 minutes or until they are cooked through and the skin is crispy.
7. While the chicken wings are still hot, drizzle the remaining spicy honey lime glaze over them.
8. Serve the Spicy Honey Lime Air-Fried Chicken Wings with your favourite dipping sauce.

# Kentucky Air Fried Chicken Wings

**Serves: 4**
**Prep time: 10 minutes / Cook time: 30 minutes**

Kentucky fried chicken wings make for a great appetiser or as part of a main dish. This recipe is a healthier variant of the deep fried variant

## Ingredients:

- 1400g of chicken wings (15-16 wings)
- 350ml buttermilk
- 2 large eggs
- 240g all-purpose flour
- 3 tsp paprika
- 2 tsp garlic powder
- 2 tsp onion powder
- 2 tsp salt
- 1 tsp ground black pepper
- 1cal olive oil spray

## Preparation Instructions

1. Preheat the air fryer at 180°C for 3-4 minutes
2. Amalgamate the buttermilk and eggs in a stand mixer
3. Using a small bowl, combine all of the dry Ingredients to make the coating flour
4. Employing some kitchen tongs, submerge each chicken wings in the flour, followed by the buttermilk, then back into the flour
5. Place the chicken in the air fryer and cover it with the fry spray
6. Preferably select the 'air crisp' function or cook the chicken at 180°C for 20 minutes
7. Shake the chicken wings and cook for another 5

minutes
8. Retrieve the chicken wings and place them into a dish, then serve

## Buttermilk-Fried Drumsticks

**Serves: 2**
**Prep time: 10 minutes / Cook time: 25 minutes**

### Ingredients:
- 1 egg
- 120 g buttermilk
- 90 g self-rising flour
- 90 g seasoned panko bread crumbs
- 1 teaspoon salt
- ¼ teaspoon ground black pepper (to mix into coating)
- 4 chicken drumsticks, skin on
- Oil for misting or cooking spray

### Preparation instructions:
1. Beat together egg and buttermilk in shallow dish.
2. In a second shallow dish, combine the flour, panko crumbs, salt, and pepper.
3. Sprinkle chicken legs with additional salt and pepper to taste.
4. Dip legs in buttermilk mixture, then roll in panko mixture, pressing in crumbs to make coating stick. Mist with oil or cooking spray.
5. Spray the air fryer basket with cooking spray.
6. Cook drumsticks at 180°C for 10 minutes. Turn pieces over and cook an additional 10 minutes.
7. Turn pieces to check for browning. If you have any white spots that haven't begun to brown, spritz them with oil or cooking spray. Continue cooking for 5 more minutes or until crust is golden brown and juices run clear. Larger, meatier drumsticks will take longer to cook than small ones.

## Sriracha-Honey Chicken Nuggets

**Serves: 6**
**Prep time: 15 minutes / Cook time: 19 minutes**

### Ingredients:
- Oil, for spraying
- 1 large egg
- 180 ml milk
- 125 g all-purpose flour
- 2 tablespoons icing sugar
- ½ teaspoon paprika
- ½ teaspoon salt
- ½ teaspoon freshly ground black pepper
- 2 boneless, skinless chicken breasts, cut into bite-size pieces
- 140 g barbecue sauce
- 2 tablespoons honey
- 1 tablespoon Sriracha

### Preparation instructions:
1. Line the air fryer basket with parchment and spray lightly with oil.
2. In a small bowl, whisk together the egg and milk.
3. In a medium bowl, combine the flour, icing sugar, paprika, salt, and black pepper and stir.
4. Coat the chicken in the egg mixture, then dredge in the flour mixture until evenly coated.
5. Place the chicken in the prepared basket and spray liberally with oil.
6. Air fry at 200°C for 8 minutes, flip, spray with more oil, and cook for another 6 to 8 minutes, or until the internal temperature reaches 76°C and the juices run clear.
7. In a large bowl, mix together the barbecue sauce, honey, and Sriracha.
8. Transfer the chicken to the bowl and toss until well coated with the barbecue sauce mixture.
9. Line the air fryer basket with fresh parchment, return the chicken to the basket, and cook for another 2 to 3 minutes, until browned and crispy.

## Air Fryer Chicken-Fried Steak

**Serves: 6**
**Prep time: 15 minutes / Cook time: 19 minutes**

### Ingredients:
- 450 g beef braising steak
- 700 ml low-fat milk, divided
- 1 teaspoon dried thyme
- 1 teaspoon dried rosemary
- 2 medium egg whites
- 235 ml gluten-free breadcrumbs
- 120 ml coconut flour
- 1 tablespoon Cajun seasoning

### Preparation instructions:
1. In a bowl, marinate the steak in 475 ml of milk for 30 to 45 minutes.
2. Remove the steak from milk, shake off the excess liquid, and season with the thyme and rosemary. Discard the milk.
3. In a shallow bowl, beat the egg whites with the remaining 235 ml of milk.
4. In a separate shallow bowl, combine the breadcrumbs, coconut flour, and seasoning.
5. Dip the steak in the egg white mixture then dredge in the breadcrumb mixture, coating well.
6. Place the steak in the basket of an air fryer.
7. Set the air fryer to 200°C, close, and cook for 10 minutes.
8. Open the air fryer, turn the steaks, close, and cook for 10 minutes. Let rest for 5 minutes.

# Chapter 4: Beef, Pork & Lamb

## Korean BBQ Air-Fried Beef Bulgogi Sliders

Serves: 4
Prep time: 15 minutes / Cook time: 10 minutes

### Ingredients:
- 400g beef sirloin or ribeye, thinly sliced
- 60ml Korean BBQ sauce
- 1 tbsp soy sauce
- 1 tbsp sesame oil
- 1 tsp grated ginger
- 2 cloves garlic, minced
- Salt and black pepper, to taste
- 4 slider buns
- Thinly sliced cucumber and lettuce leaves, for garnish

### Preparation instructions:
1. In a bowl, mix together the Korean BBQ sauce, soy sauce, sesame oil, grated ginger, minced garlic, salt, and black pepper to make the marinade.
2. Add the thinly sliced beef to the marinade and toss it to coat evenly. Let it marinate for about 10 minutes.
3. Preheat the Air Fryer to 200°C for 5 minutes.
4. Grease the Air Fryer basket with a little cooking spray or vegetable oil.
5. Arrange the marinated beef slices in the Air Fryer basket in a single layer.
6. Air fry the beef at 200°C for 6-8 minutes or until it is cooked through and slightly charred.
7. Toast the slider buns in the Air Fryer for about 1-2 minutes until they are lightly toasted.
8. Assemble the Korean BBQ Air-Fried Beef Bulgogi Sliders by placing the cooked beef on the slider buns and garnishing with thinly sliced cucumber and lettuce leaves.

## Crispy Garlic Parmesan Air-Fried Pork Tenderloin Medallions

Serves: 4
Prep time: 15 minutes / Cook time: 12 minutes

### Ingredients:
- 400g pork tenderloin, sliced into medallions
- 60ml buttermilk
- 100g breadcrumbs
- 50g grated Parmesan cheese
- 2 garlic cloves, minced
- 1 tsp dried thyme
- 1/2 tsp paprika
- Salt and black pepper, to taste
- Cooking spray or vegetable oil

### Preparation instructions:
1. In a bowl, marinate the pork tenderloin medallions in buttermilk for about 10 minutes.
2. In another bowl, mix together the breadcrumbs, grated Parmesan cheese, minced garlic, dried thyme, paprika, salt, and black pepper to make the coating mixture.
3. Dip each marinated pork medallion into the breadcrumb mixture, pressing the breadcrumbs onto the pork to adhere.
4. Preheat the Air Fryer to 200°C for 5 minutes.
5. Grease the Air Fryer basket with a little cooking spray or vegetable oil.
6. Arrange the coated pork medallions in the Air Fryer basket in a single layer.
7. Air fry the pork medallions at 200°C for 10-12 minutes or until they are cooked through and the coating is crispy and golden brown.
8. Serve the Crispy Garlic Parmesan Air-Fried Pork Tenderloin Medallions with your favourite side dishes.

## Moroccan Spiced Air-Fried Lamb Meatballs

Serves: 4
Prep time: 20 minutes / Cook time: 12 minutes

### Ingredients:
- 500g minced lamb
- 1 small onion, finely chopped
- 2 garlic cloves, minced
- 2 tbsp chopped fresh parsley
- 1 tsp ground cumin
- 1 tsp ground coriander
- 1/2 tsp ground cinnamon
- 1/4 tsp ground ginger
- 1/4 tsp ground paprika
- Salt and black pepper, to taste
- Cooking spray or vegetable oil

### Preparation instructions:
1. In a bowl, mix together the minced lamb, finely chopped onion, minced garlic, chopped fresh parsley, ground cumin, ground coriander, ground cinnamon, ground ginger, ground paprika, salt, and black pepper to make the lamb meatball mixture.
2. Shape the mixture into small meatballs.
3. Preheat the Air Fryer to 200°C for 5 minutes.
4. Grease the Air Fryer basket with a little cooking

spray or vegetable oil.
5. Arrange the lamb meatballs in the Air Fryer basket in a single layer.
6. Air fry the lamb meatballs at 200°C for 10-12 minutes or until they are cooked through and slightly browned.
7. Serve the Moroccan Spiced Air-Fried Lamb Meatballs with couscous and a yoghurt dip.

## Teriyaki Pineapple Air-Fried Beef Skewers

**Serves: 4**
**Prep time: 30 minutes / Cook time: 10 minutes**

### Ingredients:
- 500g beef sirloin or ribeye, cut into bite-sized pieces
- 60ml teriyaki sauce
- 2 tbsp soy sauce
- 2 tbsp honey
- 1 tsp grated ginger
- 1 garlic clove, minced
- Salt and black pepper, to taste
- 200g pineapple chunks
- Wooden skewers, soaked in water for 30 minutes

### Preparation instructions:
1. In a bowl, mix together the teriyaki sauce, soy sauce, honey, grated ginger, minced garlic, salt, and black pepper to make the teriyaki marinade.
2. Add the beef pieces to the teriyaki marinade and toss them to coat evenly. Let them marinate for about 20 minutes.
3. Preheat the Air Fryer to 200°C for 5 minutes.
4. Thread the marinated beef pieces and pineapple chunks onto the soaked wooden skewers.
5. Grease the Air Fryer basket with a little cooking spray or vegetable oil.
6. Arrange the beef skewers in the Air Fryer basket in a single layer.
7. Air fry the teriyaki pineapple beef skewers at 200°C for 8-10 minutes or until the beef is cooked to your desired level of doneness and the pineapple is slightly caramelised.
8. Serve the Teriyaki Pineapple Air-Fried Beef Skewers with steamed rice and stir-fried vegetables.

## BBQ Pulled Pork-Stuffed Air-Fried Jalapenos

**Serves: 4**
**Prep time: 30 minutes / Cook time: 12 minutes**

### Ingredients:
- 8 large jalapeno peppers
- 200g cooked pulled pork
- 60ml barbecue sauce
- 100g cream cheese, softened
- 60g shredded cheddar cheese
- Salt and black pepper, to taste
- Cooking spray or vegetable oil

### Preparation instructions:
1. Preheat the Air Fryer to 200°C for 5 minutes.
2. Cut the jalapeno peppers in half lengthwise and remove the seeds and membranes.
3. In a bowl, mix together the cooked pulled pork and barbecue sauce to make the pulled pork filling.
4. In another bowl, mix together the softened cream cheese, shredded cheddar cheese, salt, and black pepper to make the cheese filling. Spoon the pulled pork filling into each jalapeno half.
5. Top the pulled pork filling with the cheese filling, pressing it down gently.
6. Grease the Air Fryer basket with a little cooking spray or vegetable oil.
7. Arrange the stuffed jalapenos in the Air Fryer basket in a single layer.
8. Air fry the BBQ Pulled Pork-Stuffed Air-Fried Jalapenos at 200°C for 10-12 minutes or until the jalapenos are tender and the cheese is melted and slightly browned.
9. Serve the stuffed jalapenos as a delicious appetiser or snack.

## Rosemary and Garlic Air-Fried Lamb Chops

**Serves: 4**
**Prep time: 15 minutes / Cook time: 12 minutes**

### Ingredients:
- 8 lamb chops
- 60ml olive oil
- 2 garlic cloves, minced
- 2 tbsp chopped fresh rosemary
- Salt and black pepper, to taste
- Cooking spray or vegetable oil

### Preparation instructions:
1. In a bowl, mix together the olive oil, minced garlic, chopped fresh rosemary, salt, and black pepper to make the rosemary and garlic marinade.
2. Add the lamb chops to the marinade and toss them to coat evenly. Let them marinate for about 10 minutes.
3. Preheat the Air Fryer to 200°C for 5 minutes.
4. Grease the Air Fryer basket with a little cooking spray or vegetable oil.
5. Arrange the marinated lamb chops in the Air Fryer basket in a single layer.
6. Air fry the lamb chops at 200°C for 10-12 minutes

or until they are cooked to your desired level of doneness and slightly browned.
7. Serve the Rosemary and Garlic Air-Fried Lamb Chops with roasted vegetables and mashed potatoes.

## Tex-Mex Air-Fried Beef Taquitos with Avocado Dip

**Serves: 4**
**Prep time: 30 minutes / Cook time: 10 minutes**

### Ingredients:

- 400g beef mince
- 1 small onion, finely chopped
- 1 red bell pepper, finely diced
- 2 garlic cloves, minced
- 2 tbsp Tex-Mex seasoning (shop-bought or homemade)
- 60ml water
- Salt and black pepper, to taste
- 8 small flour tortillas
- Cooking spray or vegetable oil

**Avocado Dip:**

- 1 ripe avocado, peeled and pitted
- 60ml Greek yoghurt
- 60ml chopped fresh coriander
- 1 lime, juiced
- Salt and black pepper, to taste

### Preparation instructions:

1. In a pan, cook the beef mince over medium heat until it is browned and cooked through.
2. Add the finely chopped onion, diced red bell pepper, minced garlic, Tex-Mex seasoning, water, salt, and black pepper to the cooked beef mince. Stir to combine and let it simmer for a few minutes until the vegetables are tender and the flavors are well combined.
3. Preheat the Air Fryer to 200°C for 5 minutes. Warm the flour tortillas in the microwave or in a pan to make them pliable.
4. Spoon the Tex-Mex beef filling onto each tortilla and roll it up tightly to form the taquitos. Secure the taquitos with toothpicks if needed.
5. Grease the Air Fryer basket with a little cooking spray or vegetable oil.
6. Arrange the beef taquitos in the Air Fryer basket in a single layer.
7. Air fry the Tex-Mex Air-Fried Beef Taquitos at 200°C for 8-10 minutes or until they are crispy and golden brown.
8. For the avocado dip, blend the peeled and pitted avocado, Greek yoghurt, chopped fresh coriander, lime juice, salt, and black pepper until smooth and creamy.
9. Serve the Tex-Mex Air-Fried Beef Taquitos with the avocado dip and enjoy!

## Italian Herb Air-Fried Pork Milanese

**Serves: 4**
**Prep time: 20 minutes / Cook time: 12 minutes**

### Ingredients:

- 400g pork loin, thinly sliced
- 60ml buttermilk
- 240 g breadcrumbs
- 2 tbsp grated Parmesan cheese
- 1 tbsp chopped fresh parsley
- 1 tsp dried oregano
- 1/2 tsp garlic powder
- Salt and black pepper, to taste
- Cooking spray or vegetable oil

### Preparation instructions:

1. In a bowl, marinate the thinly sliced pork loin in buttermilk for about 10 minutes.
2. In another bowl, mix together the breadcrumbs, grated Parmesan cheese, chopped fresh parsley, dried oregano, garlic powder, salt, and black pepper to make the coating mixture.
3. Dip each marinated pork slice into the breadcrumb mixture, pressing the breadcrumbs onto the pork to adhere.
4. Preheat the Air Fryer to 200°C for 5 minutes.
5. Grease the Air Fryer basket with a little cooking spray or vegetable oil.
6. Arrange the coated pork slices in the Air Fryer basket in a single layer.
7. Air fry the Italian Herb Air-Fried Pork Milanese at 200°C for 10-12 minutes or until it is cooked through and the coating is crispy and golden brown.
8. Serve the Italian Herb Air-Fried Pork Milanese with a side of salad or pasta.

## Spicy Szechuan Air-Fried Beef Stir-Fry

**Serves: 4**
**Prep time: 30 minutes / Cook time: 10 minutes**

### Ingredients:

- 500g beef sirloin or ribeye, thinly sliced
- 60ml soy sauce
- 2 tbsp hoisin sauce
- 2 tbsp rice vinegar
- 1 tbsp Szechuan peppercorns, crushed
- 1 tbsp sesame oil
- 2 garlic cloves, minced
- 2 cm piece of ginger, grated
- 1 red pepper, thinly sliced
- 1 yellow pepper, thinly sliced
- 1 green pepper, thinly sliced

- 2 spring onions, thinly sliced
- Cooking spray or vegetable oil

**Preparation instructions:**

1. In a bowl, mix together the soy sauce, hoisin sauce, rice vinegar, crushed Szechuan peppercorns, sesame oil, minced garlic, and grated ginger to make the spicy Szechuan marinade.
2. Add the thinly sliced beef to the marinade and toss it to coat evenly. Let it marinate for about 20 minutes.
3. Preheat the Air Fryer to 200°C for 5 minutes.
4. Grease the Air Fryer basket with a little cooking spray or vegetable oil.
5. Arrange the marinated beef slices, bell pepper slices, and spring onions in the Air Fryer basket in a single layer.
6. Air fry the Spicy Szechuan Air-Fried Beef Stir-Fry at 200°C for 8-10 minutes or until the beef is cooked through and the vegetables are tender-crisp.
7. Serve the Spicy Szechuan Air-Fried Beef Stir-Fry over steamed rice or noodles.

## Mediterranean Stuffed Air-Fried Lamb Burgers

**Serves: 4**
**Prep time: 20 minutes / Cook time: 12 minutes**

**Ingredients:**

- 500g minced lamb
- 1 small onion, finely chopped
- 2 garlic cloves, minced
- 2 tbsp chopped fresh parsley
- 2 tbsp chopped fresh mint
- 1 tsp ground cumin
- 1 tsp ground coriander
- Salt and black pepper, to taste
- 60g feta cheese, crumbled
- 4 burger buns
- Lettuce leaves, sliced tomatoes, and sliced red onions, for garnish
- Cooking spray or vegetable oil

**Preparation instructions:**

1. In a bowl, mix together the ground lamb, finely chopped onion, minced garlic, chopped fresh parsley, chopped fresh mint, ground cumin, ground coriander, salt, and black pepper to make the lamb burger mixture.
2. Shape the mixture into 4 equal-sized patties.
3. Make an indentation in the centre of each patty and stuff it with crumbled feta cheese, then seal the edges to enclose the cheese.
4. Preheat the Air Fryer to 200°C for 5 minutes.
5. Grease the Air Fryer basket with a little cooking spray or vegetable oil.
6. Arrange the stuffed lamb burgers in the Air Fryer basket in a single layer.
7. Air fry the Mediterranean Stuffed Air-Fried Lamb Burgers at 200°C for 10-12 minutes or until they are cooked to your desired level of doneness.
8. Toast the burger buns in the Air Fryer for about 1-2 minutes until they are lightly toasted.
9. Assemble the lamb burgers by placing each patty on a toasted bun and garnishing with lettuce leaves, sliced tomatoes, and sliced red onions.

## Honey Mustard Glazed Air-Fried Pork Belly Bites

**Serves: 4**
**Prep time: 20 minutes / Cook time: 20 minutes**

**Ingredients:**

- 400g pork belly, cut into bite-sized pieces
- 2 tbsp honey
- 2 tbsp Dijon mustard
- 2 tbsp soy sauce
- 1 tbsp olive oil
- 1/2 tsp garlic powder
- Salt and black pepper, to taste
- Cooking spray or vegetable oil

**Preparation instructions:**

1. In a bowl, mix together the honey, Dijon mustard, soy sauce, olive oil, garlic powder, salt, and black pepper to make the honey mustard glaze.
2. Add the pork belly pieces to the honey mustard glaze and toss them to coat evenly. Let them marinate for about 10 minutes.
3. Preheat the Air Fryer to 200°C for 5 minutes.
4. Grease the Air Fryer basket with a little cooking spray or vegetable oil.
5. Arrange the marinated pork belly bites in the Air Fryer basket in a single layer.
6. Air fry the pork belly bites at 200°C for 18-20 minutes or until they are cooked through and crispy.
7. Serve the Honey Mustard Glazed Air-Fried Pork Belly Bites as a delicious appetiser or snack.

## Mongolian-Style Air-Fried Beef and Broccoli

**Serves: 4**
**Prep time: 15 minutes / Cook time: 15 minutes**

**Ingredients:**

- 400g beef sirloin, thinly sliced
- 2 tbsp soy sauce
- 2 tbsp hoisin sauce

- 2 tbsp oyster sauce
- 2 tbsp brown sugar
- 1 tbsp cornstarch
- 2 tbsp vegetable oil
- 2 garlic cloves, minced
- 1 cm piece of ginger, grated
- 1 broccoli head, cut into florets
- Salt and black pepper, to taste
- Cooking spray or vegetable oil

**Preparation instructions:**

1. In a bowl, mix together the soy sauce, hoisin sauce, oyster sauce, brown sugar, and cornstarch to make the Mongolian-style sauce.
2. Add the thinly sliced beef to the sauce and toss it to coat evenly. Let it marinate for about 10 minutes. Preheat the Air Fryer to 200°C for 5 minutes.
3. Grease the Air Fryer basket with a little cooking spray or vegetable oil.
4. Heat 1 tablespoon of vegetable oil in a pan over medium heat. Stir-fry the minced garlic and grated ginger until fragrant.
5. Add the marinated beef to the pan and stir-fry until it is cooked through and slightly caramelised. Set aside.
6. In the same pan, heat the remaining tablespoon of vegetable oil and stir-fry the broccoli florets until they are tender-crisp.
7. Return the cooked beef to the pan with the broccoli, and stir in the Mongolian-style sauce. Cook for a few more minutes until the sauce thickens and coats the beef and broccoli.
8. Transfer the Mongolian-Style Air-Fried Beef and Broccoli to the Air Fryer basket and air fry at 200°C for 2-3 minutes to get a nice char on the beef and broccoli.
9. Serve the Mongolian-Style Air-Fried Beef and Broccoli over steamed rice.

## Greek Lemon Garlic Air-Fried Lamb Chops

**Serves: 4**
**Prep time: 10 minutes / Cook time: 12 minutes**

**Ingredients:**

- 8 lamb chops
- 60ml olive oil
- 3 garlic cloves, minced
- 1 lemon, juiced and zested
- 2 tbsp chopped fresh oregano
- Salt and black pepper, to taste
- Cooking spray or vegetable oil

**Preparation instructions:**

1. In a bowl, mix together the olive oil, minced garlic, lemon juice and zest, chopped fresh oregano, salt, and black pepper to make the Greek lemon garlic marinade.
2. Add the lamb chops to the marinade and toss them to coat evenly. Let them marinate for about 10 minutes.
3. Preheat the Air Fryer to 200°C for 5 minutes.
4. Grease the Air Fryer basket with a little cooking spray or vegetable oil.
5. Arrange the marinated lamb chops in the Air Fryer basket in a single layer.
6. Air fry the Greek Lemon Garlic Air-Fried Lamb Chops at 200°C for 10-12 minutes or until they are cooked to your desired level of doneness and slightly browned.
7. Serve the Greek Lemon Garlic Air-Fried Lamb Chops with a side of Greek salad or roasted vegetables.

## Jamaican Jerk Air-Fried Pork Ribs

**Serves: 4**
**Prep time: 20 minutes / Cook time: 35 minutes**

**Ingredients:**

- 800g pork ribs
- 2 tbsp Jamaican jerk seasoning (store-bought or homemade)
- 2 tbsp vegetable oil
- 1 lime, juiced
- Salt and black pepper, to taste
- Cooking spray or vegetable oil

**Preparation instructions:**

1. In a bowl, mix together the Jamaican jerk seasoning, vegetable oil, lime juice, salt, and black pepper to make the jerk marinade.
2. Rub the marinade all over the pork ribs, making sure they are evenly coated. Let them marinate for about 15 minutes.
3. Preheat the Air Fryer to 180°C for 5 minutes.
4. Grease the Air Fryer basket with a little cooking spray or vegetable oil.
5. Arrange the marinated pork ribs in the Air Fryer basket in a single layer.
6. Air fry the Jamaican Jerk Air-Fried Pork Ribs at 180°C for 30-35 minutes or until they are tender and the surface is slightly charred.
7. Serve the Jamaican Jerk Air-Fried Pork Ribs with rice and beans or coleslaw.

## Spinach and Feta Stuffed Air-Fried Beef Roll-Ups

**Serves: 4**
**Prep time: 20 minutes / Cook time: 12 minutes**

**Ingredients:**

- 4 beef minute steaks

- 100g fresh spinach leaves
- 100g feta cheese, crumbled
- 1 tbsp olive oil
- 1 garlic clove, minced
- Salt and black pepper, to taste
- Cooking spray or vegetable oil

**Preparation instructions:**

1. Preheat the Air Fryer to 200°C for 5 minutes.
2. In a pan, heat the olive oil over medium heat and sauté the minced garlic until fragrant.
3. Add the fresh spinach leaves to the pan and cook until they wilt. Season with salt and black pepper.
4. Lay out each beef minute steak and place a portion of the sautéed spinach and crumbled feta cheese on one end of each steak.
5. Roll up the beef steaks, enclosing the spinach and feta filling, and secure them with toothpicks if needed.
6. Grease the Air Fryer basket with a little cooking spray or vegetable oil.
7. Arrange the stuffed beef roll-ups in the Air Fryer basket in a single layer.
8. Air fry the Spinach and Feta Stuffed Air-Fried Beef Roll-Ups at 200°C for 10-12 minutes or until the beef is cooked through and slightly browned.
9. Serve the Spinach and Feta Stuffed Air-Fried Beef Roll-Ups with a side of roasted vegetables or a Greek salad.

## Apricot Glazed Air-Fried Lamb Steaks

Serves: 4
Prep time: 15 minutes / Cook time: 12 minutes

**Ingredients:**

- 4 lamb steaks
- 60ml apricot jam
- 2 tbsp soy sauce
- 2 tbsp Dijon mustard
- 1 tbsp balsamic vinegar
- 2 garlic cloves, minced
- Salt and black pepper, to taste
- Cooking spray or vegetable oil

**Preparation instructions:**

1. In a bowl, mix together the apricot jam, soy sauce, Dijon mustard, balsamic vinegar, minced garlic, salt, and black pepper to make the apricot glaze.
2. Add the lamb steaks to the glaze and toss them to coat evenly. Let them marinate for about 10 minutes.
3. Preheat the Air Fryer to 200°C for 5 minutes.
4. Grease the Air Fryer basket with a little cooking spray or vegetable oil.
5. Arrange the marinated lamb steaks in the Air Fryer basket in a single layer.
6. Air fry the Apricot Glazed Air-Fried Lamb Steaks at 200°C for 10-12 minutes or until they are cooked to your desired level of doneness and the glaze is slightly caramelised.
7. Serve the Apricot Glazed Air-Fried Lamb Steaks with couscous or quinoa and steamed vegetables.

## Panko-Crusted Air-Fried Pork Schnitzel

Serves: 4
Prep time: 20 minutes / Cook time: 12 minutes

**Ingredients:**

- 4 pork schnitzels (thinly pounded pork chops)
- 60ml buttermilk
- 100g panko breadcrumbs
- 2 tbsp grated Parmesan cheese
- 1 tsp paprika
- 1/2 tsp garlic powder
- Salt and black pepper, to taste
- Cooking spray or vegetable oil

**Preparation instructions:**

1. In a shallow bowl, pour the buttermilk and add the pork schnitzels, turning them to coat both sides. Let them marinate for about 10 minutes.
2. In another shallow bowl, mix together the panko breadcrumbs, grated Parmesan cheese, paprika, garlic powder, salt, and black pepper to make the coating mixture.
3. Remove the pork schnitzels from the buttermilk, allowing any excess liquid to drip off, and then coat them in the panko mixture, pressing the breadcrumbs onto the pork to adhere.
4. Preheat the Air Fryer to 200°C for 5 minutes.
5. Grease the Air Fryer basket with a little cooking spray or vegetable oil.
6. Arrange the coated pork schnitzels in the Air Fryer basket in a single layer.
7. Air fry the Panko-Crusted Air-Fried Pork Schnitzel at 200°C for 10-12 minutes or until they are cooked through and the coating is crispy and golden brown.
8. Serve the Panko-Crusted Air-Fried Pork Schnitzel with a squeeze of lemon and a side of potato salad or coleslaw.

## Mexican Street Corn Air-Fried Beef Tacos

Serves: 4
Prep time: 20 minutes / Cook time: 10 minutes

**Ingredients:**

- 400g beef mince

- 1 tbsp vegetable oil
- 1 tsp chilli powder
- 1 tsp ground cumin
- 1/2 tsp smoked paprika
- 1/4 tsp cayenne pepper (optional, for extra heat)
- 2 garlic cloves, minced
- 1 lime, juiced
- Salt and black pepper, to taste
- 8 small corn tortillas
- 100g crumbled feta cheese
- Fresh coriander leaves, for garnish
- Cooking spray or vegetable oil

**Preparation instructions:**

1. In a pan, heat the vegetable oil over medium heat and sauté the minced garlic until fragrant.
2. Add the beef mince to the pan and cook until it is browned and cooked through.
3. Stir in the chilli powder, ground cumin, smoked paprika, cayenne pepper (if using), lime juice, salt, and black pepper. Cook for a few more minutes until the flavours are well combined.
4. Preheat the Air Fryer to 200°C for 5 minutes.
5. Grease the Air Fryer basket with a little cooking spray or vegetable oil.
6. Warm the corn tortillas in the microwave or in a pan to make them pliable.
7. Spoon the Mexican street corn beef filling onto each tortilla and top it with crumbled feta cheese and fresh coriander leaves.
8. Fold the tortillas in half to form the tacos, and arrange them in the Air Fryer basket in a single layer. Air fry the Mexican Street Corn Air-Fried Beef Tacos at 200°C for 2-3 minutes or until they are warmed through and slightly crispy.
9. Serve the Mexican Street Corn Air-Fried Beef Tacos with a side of salsa and lime wedges.

# Cajun Butter Air-Fried Beef and Potato Wedges

**Serves: 4**
**Prep time: 20 minutes / Cook time: 25 minutes**

### Ingredients:

- 400g beef sirloin, thinly sliced
- 500g potatoes, cut into wedges
- 60g butter, melted
- 2 tsp Cajun seasoning
- 1 tsp garlic powder
- Salt and black pepper, to taste
- Cooking spray or vegetable oil

### Preparation instructions:

1. In a bowl, mix together the melted butter, Cajun seasoning, garlic powder, salt, and black pepper to make the Cajun butter sauce.
2. Add the thinly sliced beef to the sauce and toss it to coat evenly. Let it marinate for about 10 minutes.
3. Preheat the Air Fryer to 200°C for 5 minutes.
4. Grease the Air Fryer basket with a little cooking spray or vegetable oil.
5. Arrange the marinated beef slices and potato wedges in the Air Fryer basket in a single layer.
6. Air fry the Cajun Butter Air-Fried Beef and Potato Wedges at 200°C for 20-25 minutes or until the beef is cooked through and the potato wedges are crispy and golden brown.
7. Serve the Cajun Butter Air-Fried Beef and Potato Wedges with a side of coleslaw or a green salad.

# Mediterranean Lamb Gyro Meatballs with Tzatziki Sauce

**Serves: 4**
**Prep time: 20 minutes / Cook time: 12 minutes**

### Ingredients:

- 500g minced lamb
- 1 small onion, grated
- 2 garlic cloves, minced
- 2 tbsp chopped fresh parsley
- 2 tbsp chopped fresh mint
- 1 tsp ground cumin
- 1 tsp ground coriander
- Salt and black pepper, to taste
- 4 pita breads
- Fresh lettuce, sliced tomatoes, and sliced cucumbers, for garnish
- Cooking spray or vegetable oil
- For the Tzatziki Sauce:
- 150ml Greek yoghurt
- 1/2 cucumber, grated and squeezed to remove excess moisture
- 1 garlic clove, minced
- 1 tbsp chopped fresh dill
- 1 tbsp lemon juice
- Salt and black pepper, to taste

### Preparation instructions:

1. In a bowl, mix together the ground lamb, grated onion, minced garlic, chopped fresh parsley, chopped fresh mint, ground cumin, ground coriander, salt, and black pepper to make the lamb gyro meatball mixture.
2. Shape the mixture into small meatballs, about the size of a walnut.
3. Preheat the Air Fryer to 200°C for 5 minutes.
4. Grease the Air Fryer basket with a little cooking spray or vegetable oil.

5. Arrange the lamb gyro meatballs in the Air Fryer basket in a single layer.
6. Air fry the Mediterranean Lamb Gyro Meatballs at 200°C for 10-12 minutes or until they are cooked through and slightly browned.
7. While the meatballs are cooking, prepare the Tzatziki sauce by mixing together the Greek yoghurt, grated cucumber, minced garlic, chopped fresh dill, lemon juice, salt, and black pepper in a bowl.
8. Warm the pita breads in the Air Fryer for about 1-2 minutes until they are soft and pliable.
9. Assemble the Mediterranean Lamb Gyro Meatballs by placing them in the warmed pita breads, and garnishing with fresh lettuce, sliced tomatoes, sliced cucumbers, and a generous drizzle of Tzatziki sauce.

## Bacon-Wrapped Pork Tenderloin

**Serves: 6**
**Prep time: 30 minutes / Cook time: 22 to 25 minutes**

### Ingredients:

- 120 ml minced onion
- 120 ml apple cider, or apple juice
- 60 ml honey
- 1 tablespoon minced garlic
- ¼ teaspoon salt
- ¼ teaspoon freshly ground black pepper
- 900 g pork tenderloin
- 1 to 2 tablespoons oil
- 8 uncooked bacon slices

### Preparation instructions:

1. In a medium bowl, stir together the onion, cider, honey, garlic, salt, and pepper. Transfer to a large resealable bag or airtight container and add the pork. Seal the bag. Refrigerate to marinate for at least 2 hours.
2. Preheat the air fryer to 204°C. Line the air fryer basket with parchment paper.
3. Remove the pork from the marinade and place it on the parchment. Spritz with oil.
4. Cook for 15 minutes.
5. Wrap the bacon slices around the pork and secure them with toothpicks. Turn the pork roast and spritz with oil. Cook for 7 to 10 minutes more until the internal temperature reaches 64°C, depending on how well-done you like pork loin. It will continue cooking after it's removed from the fryer, so let it sit for 5 minutes before serving.

## Beef Haslet (meatloaf)

**Serves: 4-5**
**Prep time: 10 minutes / Cook time: 20 minutes**

### Ingredients:

- 500g beef mince (80% beef)
- 125g finely chopped onion
- 1 large beaten egg
- 25g bread crumbs
- 1 tbsp chopped thyme
- 1 tsp sea salt
- 1 tsp ground black pepper
- 2 mushrooms sliced into wedges
- 1 ½ tbsp flaxseed oil

### Preparation instructions:

1. Start by preheating the air fryer at 200°C for 4-5 minutes
2. Toss the minced beef into a large bowl
3. Add the onions, bread crumbs, egg, thyme, salt and pepper
4. Hand mix and amalgamate the Ingredients
5. Dollop this meat mixture into a loaf pan to create a slab of meat
6. Peirce mushrooms into the slab of meat and brush them over with oil
7. Place the meat slab in the air fryer at 180°C for 25-30 minutes
8. Retrieve the beef haslet and set it aside to cool
9. Slice the beef haslet into 4-5 portions and serve

## Parmesan Herb Filet Mignon

**Serves: 4**
**Prep time: 20 minutes / Cook time: 13 minutes**

### Ingredients:

- 450 g filet mignon
- Sea salt and ground black pepper, to taste
- ½ teaspoon cayenne pepper
- 1 teaspoon dried basil
- 1 teaspoon dried rosemary
- 1 teaspoon dried thyme
- 1 tablespoon sesame oil
- 1 small-sized egg, well-whisked
- 120 ml Parmesan cheese, grated

### Preparation instructions:

1. Season the filet mignon with salt, black pepper, cayenne pepper, basil, rosemary, and thyme. Brush with sesame oil.
2. Put the egg in a shallow plate. Now, place the Parmesan cheese in another plate.
3. Coat the filet mignon with the egg; then lay it into the Parmesan cheese. Set the air fryer to 182°C.
4. Cook for 10 to 13 minutes or until golden. Serve with mixed salad leaves and enjoy!

# Chapter 5: Beans & Legumes

## Crispy Cajun Chickpea Snack Mix

**Serves: 4**
**Prep time: 5 minutes / Cook time: 15 minutes**

### Ingredients:
- 400g canned chickpeas, drained and rinsed
- 1 tbsp olive oil
- 1 tsp Cajun seasoning
- 1/2 tsp garlic powder
- 1/2 tsp onion powder
- Salt, to taste

### Preparation instructions:
1. Preheat the Air Fryer to 190°C for 5 minutes.
2. In a bowl, toss the chickpeas with olive oil, Cajun seasoning, garlic powder, onion powder, and salt until evenly coated.
3. Place the seasoned chickpeas in the Air Fryer basket in a single layer.
4. Air fry the Crispy Cajun Chickpea Snack Mix at 190°C for 12-15 minutes or until the chickpeas are crispy and lightly browned.
5. Once cooked, let the chickpeas cool for a few minutes before serving.

## Buffalo Ranch Air-Fried Edamame

**Serves: 4**
**Prep time: 5 minutes / Cook time: 10 minutes**

### Ingredients:
- 400g frozen edamame, thawed
- 2 tbsp hot sauce
- 1 tbsp melted butter
- 1 tbsp ranch seasoning

### Preparation instructions:
1. Preheat the Air Fryer to 190°C for 5 minutes.
2. In a bowl, mix together the hot sauce, melted butter, and ranch seasoning to make the Buffalo Ranch sauce.
3. Toss the thawed edamame with the Buffalo Ranch sauce until well coated.
4. Place the coated edamame in the Air Fryer basket in a single layer.
5. Air fry the Buffalo Ranch Air-Fried Edamame at 190°C for 8-10 minutes or until the edamame is crispy and heated through.
6. Serve the Buffalo Ranch Air-Fried Edamame as a spicy and flavorful snack.

## Za'atar Spiced Air-Fried Falafel Bites

**Serves: 4**
**Prep time: 15 minutes / Cook time: 12 minutes**

### Ingredients:
- 400g canned chickpeas, drained and rinsed
- 1 small onion, chopped
- 2 garlic cloves, minced
- 2 tbsp fresh parsley, chopped
- 1 tbsp fresh coriander, chopped
- 1 tsp ground cumin
- 1 tsp ground coriander
- 1 tsp baking powder
- 1 tbsp za'atar seasoning
- 2 tbsp all-purpose flour
- Salt and black pepper, to taste
- Cooking spray or vegetable oil

### Preparation instructions:
1. In a food processor, combine the chickpeas, chopped onion, minced garlic, fresh parsley, fresh coriander, ground cumin, ground coriander, baking powder, za'atar seasoning, all-purpose flour, salt, and black pepper.
2. Pulse the mixture until it forms a coarse paste.
3. Preheat the Air Fryer to 200°C for 5 minutes.
4. Grease the Air Fryer basket with a little cooking spray or vegetable oil.
5. Shape the falafel mixture into small bite-sized balls and place them in the Air Fryer basket in a single layer.
6. Air fry the Za'atar Spiced Air-Fried Falafel Bites at 200°C for 10-12 minutes or until they are crispy and golden brown.
7. Serve the falafel bites with tzatziki sauce or hummus as a tasty appetiser or snack.

## Tex-Mex Air-Fried Black Bean Quesadillas

**Serves: 4**
**Prep time: 10 minutes / Cook time: 8 minutes**

### Ingredients:
- 400g canned black beans, drained and rinsed
- 1/2 small onion, finely chopped
- 1/2 red pepper, diced
- 1/2 green pepper, diced
- 1 tsp ground cumin
- 1 tsp chilli powder

- Salt and black pepper, to taste
- 4 large flour tortillas
- 100g shredded cheddar cheese
- Cooking spray or vegetable oil

**Preparation instructions:**

1. In a bowl, mash the black beans with a fork until they are partially mashed but still chunky.
2. Stir in the chopped onion, diced red bell pepper, diced green bell pepper, ground cumin, chilli powder, salt, and black pepper to make the black bean filling. Preheat the Air Fryer to 200°C for 5 minutes.
3. Grease the Air Fryer basket with a little cooking spray or vegetable oil.
4. Lay a flour tortilla on a flat surface and spread a quarter of the black bean filling on half of the tortilla.
5. Sprinkle a quarter of the shredded cheddar cheese over the black bean filling. Fold the tortilla in half to form a quesadilla and press the edges together to seal it.
6. Repeat the process to make the remaining quesadillas.
7. Place the quesadillas in the Air Fryer basket in a single layer.
8. Air fry the Tex-Mex Air-Fried Black Bean Quesadillas at 200°C for 4 minutes on each side or until they are crispy and the cheese is melted.
9. Serve the quesadillas with salsa, guacamole, and sour cream for a delicious Tex-Mex meal.

## Spicy Curry Air-Fried Lentil Samosas

**Serves: 4**
**Prep time: 15 minutes / Cook time: 12 minutes**

**Ingredients:**

- 200g dried red lentils, cooked and drained
- 1 small onion, finely chopped
- 2 garlic cloves, minced
- 1 tsp curry powder
- 1/2 tsp ground turmeric
- 1/4 tsp ground cayenne pepper (optional, for extra heat)
- 2 tbsp chopped fresh coriander
- Salt and black pepper, to taste
- 8 sheets of filo pastry
- 60 ml melted butter
- Cooking spray or vegetable oil

**Preparation instructions:**

1. In a pan, sauté the finely chopped onion and minced garlic until the onion is translucent. Add the cooked red lentils, curry powder, ground turmeric, ground cayenne pepper (if using), chopped fresh coriander, salt, and black pepper to make the lentil samosa filling. Stir until well combined.
2. Preheat the Air Fryer to 190°C for 5 minutes. Lay one sheet of filo pastry on a flat surface and brush it with melted butter.
3. Place another sheet of filo pastry on top and brush it with melted butter as well. Cut the double-layered filo pastry into four equal squares.
4. Place a spoonful of the lentil samosa filling in the centre of each square.
5. Fold each square into a triangle, enclosing the filling, and press the edges together to seal it. Repeat the process to make the remaining lentil samosas.
6. Grease the Air Fryer basket with a little cooking spray or vegetable oil.
7. Place the lentil samosas in the Air Fryer basket in a single layer.
8. Air fry the Spicy Curry Air-Fried Lentil Samosas at 190°C for 10-12 minutes or until they are crispy and lightly browned.
9. Serve the lentil samosas with mango chutney or tamarind chutney as a delightful appetiser or snack.

## Garlic Parmesan Air-Fried Green Bean Fries

**Serves: 4**
**Prep time: 10 minutes / Cook time: 10 minutes**

**Ingredients:**

- 400g fresh green beans, trimmed
- 2 tbsp olive oil
- 2 garlic cloves, minced
- 60g grated Parmesan cheese
- 1/2 tsp dried thyme
- Salt and black pepper, to taste

**Preparation instructions:**

1. Preheat the Air Fryer to 200°C for 5 minutes.
2. In a bowl, toss the trimmed green beans with olive oil and minced garlic until well coated.
3. Place the coated green beans in the Air Fryer basket in a single layer.
4. Air fry the Garlic Parmesan Air-Fried Green Bean Fries at 200°C for 8-10 minutes or until the green beans are crispy and slightly browned.
5. Once cooked, sprinkle the grated Parmesan cheese and dried thyme over the green beans and toss to combine.
6. Season with salt and black pepper to taste.
7. Serve the Garlic Parmesan Air-Fried Green Bean Fries as a delicious and healthy side dish.

## Mediterranean Herb Air-Fried Fava Bean Hummus

**Serves: 4**
**Prep time: 15 minutes / Cook time: 10 minutes**

**Ingredients:**
- 400g canned fava beans, drained and rinsed
- 2 tbsp tahini
- 2 garlic cloves, minced
- 2 tbsp fresh lemon juice
- 2 tbsp olive oil
- 1 tsp dried oregano
- 1 tsp dried thyme
- Salt and black pepper, to taste

**Preparation instructions:**
1. In a food processor, combine the fava beans, tahini, minced garlic, fresh lemon juice, olive oil, dried oregano, dried thyme, salt, and black pepper.
2. Process the mixture until it reaches a smooth and creamy consistency.
3. Preheat the Air Fryer to 190°C for 5 minutes.
4. Grease the Air Fryer basket with a little cooking spray or vegetable oil.
5. Place the fava bean hummus in the Air Fryer basket in a single layer.
6. Air fry the Mediterranean Herb Air-Fried Fava Bean Hummus at 190°C for 8-10 minutes or until it is heated through.
7. Serve the fava bean hummus with pita bread, cucumber slices, and cherry tomatoes for a delightful Mediterranean-inspired appetiser.

## BBQ Ranch Air-Fried Soybeans (Roasted Corn Nuts)

**Serves: 4**
**Prep time: 5 minutes / Cook time: 15 minutes**

**Ingredients:**
- 400g frozen soybeans (edamame), thawed
- 2 tbsp barbecue sauce
- 2 tbsp ranch seasoning

**Preparation instructions:**
1. Preheat the Air Fryer to 190°C for 5 minutes.
2. In a bowl, toss the thawed soybeans with barbecue sauce and ranch seasoning until well coated.
3. Place the coated soybeans in the Air Fryer basket in a single layer.
4. Air fry the BBQ Ranch Air-Fried Soybeans at 190°C for 12-15 minutes or until they are crispy and heated through.
5. Once cooked, let the soybeans cool for a few minutes before serving.

## Cinnamon Sugar Air-Fried Sweet Potato Hummus Dipper Chips

**Serves: 4**
**Prep time: 10 minutes / Cook time: 10 minutes**

**Ingredients:**
- 2 large sweet potatoes, peeled and thinly sliced
- 1 tbsp olive oil
- 2 tbsp granulated sugar
- 1 tsp ground cinnamon

**Preparation instructions:**
1. Preheat the Air Fryer to 200°C for 5 minutes.
2. In a bowl, toss the thinly sliced sweet potatoes with olive oil until well coated.
3. Place the sweet potato slices in the Air Fryer basket in a single layer.
4. Air fry the Cinnamon Sugar Air-Fried Sweet Potato Hummus Dipper Chips at 200°C for 8-10 minutes or until they are crispy and lightly browned.
5. In a separate bowl, mix together the granulated sugar and ground cinnamon.
6. While the sweet potato chips are still warm, sprinkle them with the cinnamon sugar mixture.
7. Serve the Cinnamon Sugar Air-Fried Sweet Potato Hummus Dipper Chips with sweet potato hummus or any other dip of your choice.

## Everything Bagel Seasoned Air-Fried Chickpeas

**Serves: 4**
**Prep time: 5 minutes / Cook time: 15 minutes**

**Ingredients:**
- 400g canned chickpeas, drained and rinsed
- 1 tbsp olive oil
- 2 tbsp everything bagel seasoning

**Preparation instructions:**
1. Preheat the Air Fryer to 190°C for 5 minutes.
2. In a bowl, toss the drained and rinsed chickpeas with olive oil until well coated.
3. Sprinkle the everything bagel seasoning over the chickpeas and toss to coat evenly.
4. Place the seasoned chickpeas in the Air Fryer basket in a single layer.
5. Air fry the Everything Bagel Seasoned Air-Fried Chickpeas at 190°C for 12-15 minutes or until they are crispy and slightly browned.
6. Once cooked, let the chickpeas cool for a few minutes before serving.

## Thai Red Curry Air-Fried Red Lentil Patties

**Serves: 4**
**Prep time: 20 minutes / Cook time: 12 minutes**

### Ingredients:
- 200g dried red lentils, cooked and drained
- 1 small onion, finely chopped
- 2 garlic cloves, minced
- 1 tbsp Thai red curry paste
- 2 tbsp chopped fresh coriander
- 2 tbsp all-purpose flour
- Salt and black pepper, to taste
- Cooking spray or vegetable oil

### Preparation instructions:
1. In a bowl, mix together the cooked and drained red lentils, finely chopped onion, minced garlic, Thai red curry paste, chopped fresh coriander, all-purpose flour, salt, and black pepper to make the lentil patty mixture.
2. Preheat the Air Fryer to 200°C for 5 minutes.
3. Grease the Air Fryer basket with a little cooking spray or vegetable oil.
4. Shape the lentil patty mixture into small patties and place them in the Air Fryer basket in a single layer.
5. Air fry the Thai Red Curry Air-Fried Red Lentil Patties at 200°C for 10-12 minutes or until they are crispy and lightly browned.
6. Serve the lentil patties with a side of Thai sweet chilli sauce or cucumber-yoghurt dip.

## Chili Lime Air-Fried Split Peas

**Serves: 4**
**Prep time: 5 minutes / Cook time: 15 minutes**

### Ingredients:
- 400g dried split peas, cooked and drained
- 1 tbsp olive oil
- 1 tsp chilli powder
- 1 tsp lime zest
- Salt, to taste

### Preparation instructions:
1. Preheat the Air Fryer to 190°C for 5 minutes.
2. In a bowl, toss the cooked and drained split peas with olive oil until well coated.
3. Sprinkle the chilli powder and lime zest over the split peas and toss to coat evenly.
4. Place the seasoned split peas in the Air Fryer basket in a single layer.
5. Air fry the Chili Lime Air-Fried Split Peas at 190°C for 12-15 minutes or until they are crispy and lightly browned.
6. Season with salt to taste.
7. Once cooked, let the split peas cool for a few minutes before serving.

## Indian Spiced Air-Fried Masala Vada (Lentil Fritters)

**Serves: 4**
**Prep time: 20 minutes / Cook time: 12 minutes**

### Ingredients:
- 200g dried chana dal (split chickpeas), soaked and drained
- 1 small onion, finely chopped
- 2 green chilies, finely chopped
- 1-inch piece of ginger, grated
- 2 tbsp chopped fresh coriander
- 1 tsp fennel seeds
- 1 tsp cumin seeds
- 1/2 tsp ground coriander
- 1/2 tsp ground turmeric
- 1/4 tsp baking soda
- Salt, to taste
- Cooking spray or vegetable oil

### Preparation instructions:
1. In a food processor, grind the soaked and drained chana dal to a coarse paste without adding water.
2. In a bowl, mix together the ground chana dal, finely chopped onion, finely chopped green chilies, grated ginger, chopped fresh coriander, fennel seeds, cumin seeds, ground coriander, ground turmeric, baking soda, and salt to make the masala vada mixture.
3. Preheat the Air Fryer to 200°C for 5 minutes.
4. Grease the Air Fryer basket with a little cooking spray or vegetable oil.
5. Shape the masala vada mixture into small flat patties and place them in the Air Fryer basket in a single layer.
6. Air fry the Indian Spiced Air-Fried Masala Vada (Lentil Fritters) at 200°C for 10-12 minutes or until they are crispy and lightly browned.
7. Serve the masala vada with coconut chutney or tomato chutney for a delicious Indian snack.

## Truffle Rosemary Air-Fried Pinto Beans

**Serves: 4**
**Prep time: 5 minutes / Cook time: 15 minutes**

### Ingredients:
- 400g canned pinto beans, drained and rinsed
- 2 tbsp truffle oil

- 1 tbsp fresh rosemary, chopped
- Salt and black pepper, to taste

**Preparation instructions:**
1. Preheat the Air Fryer to 200°C for 5 minutes.
2. In a bowl, toss the drained and rinsed pinto beans with truffle oil and chopped fresh rosemary until well coated.
3. Place the seasoned pinto beans in the Air Fryer basket in a single layer.
4. Air fry the Truffle Rosemary Air-Fried Pinto Beans at 200°C for 12-15 minutes or until they are crispy and slightly browned.
5. Season with salt and black pepper to taste.
6. Once cooked, let the pinto beans cool for a few minutes before serving.

## Za'atar Spiced Air-Fried Broad Beans

**Serves: 4**
**Prep time: 5 minutes / Cook time: 15 minutes**

**Ingredients:**
- 400g frozen broad beans, thawed
- 2 tbsp olive oil
- 1 tbsp za'atar seasoning
- Salt, to taste

**Preparation instructions:**
1. Preheat the Air Fryer to 190°C for 5 minutes.
2. In a bowl, toss the thawed broad beans with olive oil until well coated.
3. Sprinkle the za'atar seasoning over the broad beans and toss to coat evenly.
4. Place the seasoned broad beans in the Air Fryer basket in a single layer.
5. Air fry the Za'atar Spiced Air-Fried Broad Beans at 190°C for 12-15 minutes or until they are crispy and lightly browned.
6. Season with salt to taste.
7. Once cooked, let the broad beans cool for a few minutes before serving.

## Greek Herb Air-Fried Gigante Beans

**Serves: 4**
**Prep time: 5 minutes / Cook time: 15 minutes**

**Ingredients:**
- 400g canned gigante beans, drained and rinsed
- 2 tbsp olive oil
- 1 tsp dried oregano
- 1 tsp dried thyme
- 1/2 tsp dried rosemary
- Salt and black pepper, to taste

**Preparation instructions:**
1. Preheat the Air Fryer to 200°C for 5 minutes.
2. In a bowl, toss the drained and rinsed gigante beans with olive oil until well coated.
3. Sprinkle the dried oregano, dried thyme, dried rosemary, salt, and black pepper over the gigante beans and toss to coat evenly.
4. Place the seasoned gigante beans in the Air Fryer basket in a single layer.
5. Air fry the Greek Herb Air-Fried Gigante Beans at 200°C for 12-15 minutes or until they are crispy and slightly browned.
6. Once cooked, let the gigante beans cool for a few minutes before serving.

## Coconut Curry Air-Fried Chana Chaat

**Serves: 4**
**Prep time: 10 minutes / Cook time: 10 minutes**

**Ingredients:**
- 400g canned chickpeas, drained and rinsed
- 2 tbsp coconut milk
- 1 tsp curry powder
- 1/2 tsp ground cumin
- 1/2 tsp ground coriander
- 1/4 tsp turmeric powder
- Salt and black pepper, to taste
- Fresh coriander leaves, for garnish
- Lime wedges, for serving

**Preparation instructions:**
1. Preheat the Air Fryer to 190°C for 5 minutes.
2. In a bowl, toss the drained and rinsed chickpeas with coconut milk, curry powder, ground cumin, ground coriander, turmeric powder, salt, and black pepper until well coated.
3. Place the seasoned chickpeas in the Air Fryer basket in a single layer.
4. Air fry the Coconut Curry Air-Fried Chana Chaat at 190°C for 8-10 minutes or until they are crispy and lightly browned.
5. Garnish with fresh coriander leaves.
6. Serve the chana chaat with lime wedges for added flavour.

## Spicy Ranch Air-Fried Lentil Crunchies

**Serves: 4**
**Prep time: 5 minutes / Cook time: 15 minutes**

**Ingredients:**
- 200g dried red lentils, cooked and drained
- 2 tbsp olive oil
- 2 tsp ranch seasoning
- 1/2 tsp chilli powder
- Salt, to taste

**Preparation instructions:**
1. Preheat the Air Fryer to 200°C for 5 minutes.
2. In a bowl, toss the cooked and drained lentils with olive oil until well coated.
3. Sprinkle the ranch seasoning and chilli powder over the lentils and toss to coat evenly.
4. Place the seasoned lentils in the Air Fryer basket in a single layer.
5. Air fry the Spicy Ranch Air-Fried Lentil Crunchies at 200°C for 12-15 minutes or until they are crispy and lightly browned.
6. Season with salt to taste.
7. Once cooked, let the lentil crunchies cool for a few minutes before serving.

## Moroccan Harissa Air-Fried Chickpea Croquettes

**Serves: 4**
**Prep time: 15 minutes / Cook time: 12 minutes**

**Ingredients:**
- 400g canned chickpeas, drained and rinsed
- 2 tbsp harissa paste
- 2 tbsp chopped fresh coriander
- 1 tsp ground cumin
- 1/2 tsp ground coriander
- 1/4 tsp cayenne pepper (optional)
- Salt and black pepper, to taste
- Bread crumbs, for coating
- Cooking spray or vegetable oil

**Preparation instructions:**
1. In a food processor, blend the drained and rinsed chickpeas, harissa paste, chopped fresh coriander, ground cumin, ground coriander, cayenne pepper (if using), salt, and black pepper to make the chickpea croquette mixture.
2. Preheat the Air Fryer to 200°C for 5 minutes.
3. Grease your hands with a little oil, shape the chickpea mixture into small croquettes, and coat them with bread crumbs.
4. Grease the Air Fryer basket with a little cooking spray or vegetable oil.
5. Place the chickpea croquettes in the Air Fryer basket in a single layer.
6. Air fry the Moroccan Harissa Air-Fried Chickpea Croquettes at 200°C for 10-12 minutes or until they are crispy and lightly browned.
7. Once cooked, let the chickpea croquettes cool for a few minutes before serving.

## Cheesy Garlic Air-Fried Cannellini Beans

**Serves: 4**
**Prep time: 5 minutes / Cook time: 15 minutes**

**Ingredients:**
- 400g canned cannellini beans, drained and rinsed
- 2 tbsp olive oil
- 2 garlic cloves, minced
- 50g grated cheddar cheese
- Salt and black pepper, to taste

**Preparation instructions:**
1. Preheat the Air Fryer to 200°C for 5 minutes.
2. In a bowl, toss the drained and rinsed cannellini beans with olive oil and minced garlic until well coated.
3. Place the seasoned cannellini beans in the Air Fryer basket in a single layer.
4. Air fry the Cheesy Garlic Air-Fried Cannellini Beans at 200°C for 12-15 minutes or until they are crispy and slightly browned.
5. Sprinkle the grated cheddar cheese over the beans and air fry for an additional 1-2 minutes until the cheese is melted and bubbly.
6. Season with salt and black pepper to taste.
7. Once cooked, let the cannellini beans cool for a few minutes before serving.

## Crispy Chili Lime Air-Fried Black Bean Tostones

**Serves: 4**
**Prep time: 10 minutes / Cook time: 15 minutes**

**Ingredients:**
- 400g canned black beans, drained and rinsed
- 2 tbsp olive oil
- 1 tsp chilli powder
- 1/2 tsp ground cumin
- Zest of 1 lime
- Salt, to taste

**Preparation instructions:**
1. Preheat the Air Fryer to 190°C for 5 minutes.
2. In a bowl, toss the drained and rinsed black beans with olive oil until well coated.
3. Sprinkle the chilli powder, ground cumin, and lime zest over the black beans and toss to coat evenly.
4. Place the seasoned black beans in the Air Fryer basket in a single layer.

5. Air fry the Crispy Chili Lime Air-Fried Black Bean Tostones at 190°C for 12-15 minutes or until they are crispy and lightly browned.
6. Season with salt to taste.
7. Once cooked, let the black bean tostones cool for a few minutes before serving.

## Spinach and Feta Stuffed Air-Fried Mung Bean Paratha

**Serves: 4**
**Prep time: 20 minutes / Cook time: 15 minutes**

### Ingredients:
- 200g mung bean flour
- 100ml warm water
- 100g frozen chopped spinach, thawed and drained
- 100g crumbled feta cheese
- 1/2 tsp ground cumin
- 1/2 tsp ground coriander
- 1/4 tsp chilli powder
- Salt, to taste
- Cooking spray or vegetable oil

### Preparation instructions:
1. In a bowl, mix the mung bean flour with warm water to make a soft dough.
2. Knead the dough until smooth and elastic. Cover with a damp cloth and let it rest for 10 minutes.
3. In a separate bowl, mix the thawed and drained chopped spinach, crumbled feta cheese, ground cumin, ground coriander, chilli powder, and salt to make the spinach and feta filling. Preheat the Air Fryer to 200°C for 5 minutes.
4. Divide the mung bean dough into equal-sized balls and roll each ball into a small disk.
5. Place a spoonful of the spinach and feta filling in the centre of each disk. Fold the edges of the disk over the filling to form a stuffed paratha. Flatten the stuffed paratha and roll it gently to make a round flatbread.
6. Grease the Air Fryer basket with a little cooking spray or vegetable oil.
7. Place the stuffed parathas in the Air Fryer basket in a single layer.
8. Air fry the Spinach and Feta Stuffed Air-Fried Mung Bean Paratha at 200°C for 10-12 minutes or until they are crispy and lightly browned.
9. Once cooked, let the stuffed parathas cool for a few minutes before serving.

## Hawaiian Pineapple Teriyaki Air-Fried Butter Beans

**Serves: 4**
**Prep time: 5 minutes / Cook time: 15 minutes**

### Ingredients:
- 400g canned butter beans, drained and rinsed
- 2 tbsp teriyaki sauce
- 100g fresh pineapple chunks
- 1 tbsp sesame seeds
- Salt and black pepper, to taste

### Preparation instructions:
1. Preheat the Air Fryer to 190°C for 5 minutes.
2. In a bowl, toss the drained and rinsed butter beans with teriyaki sauce until well coated.
3. Add the fresh pineapple chunks to the bowl and toss with the beans.
4. Place the seasoned butter beans and pineapple in the Air Fryer basket in a single layer.
5. Air fry the Hawaiian Pineapple Teriyaki Air-Fried Butter Beans at 190°C for 12-15 minutes or until they are crispy and slightly browned.
6. Sprinkle the sesame seeds over the beans and pineapple and air fry for an additional 1-2 minutes until the seeds are toasted.
7. Season with salt and black pepper to taste.
8. Once cooked, let the butter beans and pineapple cool for a few minutes before serving.

## Simple Air Fried Crispy Brussels Sprouts

**Serves: 4**
**Prep time: 5 minutes / Cook time: 20 minutes**

### Ingredients:
- ¼ teaspoon salt
- ⅛ teaspoon ground black pepper
- 1 tablespoon extra-virgin olive oil
- 450 g Brussels sprouts, trimmed and halved
- Lemon wedges, for garnish

### Preparation instructions:
1. Preheat the air fryer to 176°C.
2. Combine the salt, black pepper, and olive oil in a large bowl. Stir to mix well.
3. Add the Brussels sprouts to the bowl of mixture and toss to coat well.
4. Arrange the Brussels sprouts in the preheated air fryer. Air fry for 20 minutes or until lightly browned and wilted. Shake the basket two times during the air frying.
5. Transfer the cooked Brussels sprouts to a large plate and squeeze the lemon wedges on top to serve.

# Chapter 6: Healthy Vegetables

## Crispy Courgette Parmesan Fries

Serves: 4
Prep time: 15 minutes / Cook time: 12 minutes

### Ingredients:
- 400g courgette, cut into fries
- 60g grated Parmesan cheese
- 60g breadcrumbs
- 1 tsp dried oregano
- 1/2 tsp garlic powder
- 1/4 tsp salt
- 1/4 tsp black pepper
- 2 large eggs, beaten

### Preparation instructions:
1. Preheat the Air Fryer to 200°C for 5 minutes.
2. In a shallow bowl, mix together the grated Parmesan cheese, breadcrumbs, dried oregano, garlic powder, salt, and black pepper.
3. Dip the courgette fries into the beaten eggs, then coat them with the Parmesan breadcrumb mixture.
4. Place the coated courgette fries in the Air Fryer basket in a single layer.
5. Air fry the Crispy courgette Parmesan Fries at 200°C for 10-12 minutes or until they are golden brown and crispy.
6. Once cooked, remove the fries from the Air Fryer and let cool for a few minutes before serving.

## Buffalo Cauliflower Bites with Blue Cheese Dip

Serves: 4
Prep time: 10 minutes / Cook time: 15 minutes

### Ingredients:
- 400g cauliflower florets
- 60ml hot sauce
- 30g butter, melted
- 1/4 tsp garlic powder
- 1/4 tsp onion powder
- Salt and black pepper, to taste
- Blue Cheese Dip:
- 120g Greek yoghurt
- 30g crumbled blue cheese
- 1 tbsp lemon juice
- 1/2 tsp dried dill
- Salt and black pepper, to taste

### Preparation instructions:
1. Preheat the Air Fryer to 190°C for 5 minutes.
2. In a bowl, mix together the hot sauce, melted butter, garlic powder, onion powder, salt, and black pepper to make the buffalo sauce.
3. Toss the cauliflower florets in the buffalo sauce until well coated.
4. Place the coated cauliflower florets in the Air Fryer basket in a single layer.
5. Air fry the Buffalo Cauliflower Bites at 190°C for 12-15 minutes or until they are crispy and slightly browned.
6. For the blue cheese dip, mix together the Greek yoghurt, crumbled blue cheese, lemon juice, dried dill, salt, and black pepper in a small bowl.
7. Once cooked, serve the Buffalo Cauliflower Bites with the blue cheese dip.

## Lemon Herb Air-Fried Asparagus Spears

Serves: 4
Prep time: 5 minutes / Cook time: 8 minutes

### Ingredients:
- 400g asparagus spears, trimmed
- 2 tbsp olive oil
- Zest of 1 lemon
- 1 tsp dried thyme
- 1 tsp dried rosemary
- Salt and black pepper, to taste

### Preparation instructions:
1. Preheat the Air Fryer to 200°C for 5 minutes.
2. In a bowl, toss the trimmed asparagus spears with olive oil until well coated.
3. Sprinkle the lemon zest, dried thyme, dried rosemary, salt, and black pepper over the asparagus and toss to coat evenly.
4. Place the seasoned asparagus spears in the Air Fryer basket in a single layer.
5. Air fry the Lemon Herb Air-Fried Asparagus Spears at 200°C for 6-8 minutes or until they are tender and lightly browned.
6. Once cooked, let the asparagus spears cool for a few minutes before serving.

## Coconut Curry Air-Fried Brussels Sprouts

Serves: 4
Prep time: 10 minutes / Cook time: 12 minutes

### Ingredients:
- 400g Brussels sprouts, halved

- 2 tbsp coconut oil, melted
- 1 tsp curry powder
- 1/2 tsp turmeric powder
- 1/4 tsp cumin powder
- 1/4 tsp chilli powder (optional)
- Salt and black pepper, to taste

**Preparation instructions:**
1. Preheat the Air Fryer to 190°C for 5 minutes.
2. In a bowl, toss the halved Brussels sprouts with melted coconut oil until well coated.
3. Sprinkle the curry powder, turmeric powder, cumin powder, chilli powder (if using), salt, and black pepper over the Brussels sprouts and toss to coat evenly.
4. Place the seasoned Brussels sprouts in the Air Fryer basket in a single layer.
5. Air fry the Coconut Curry Air-Fried Brussels Sprouts at 190°C for 10-12 minutes or until they are crispy and lightly browned.
6. Once cooked, let the Brussels sprouts cool for a few minutes before serving.

## Garlic Parmesan Air-Fried Broccoli Florets

**Serves: 4**
**Prep time: 10 minutes / Cook time: 12 minutes**

**Ingredients:**
- 400g broccoli florets
- 2 tbsp olive oil
- 2 garlic cloves, minced
- 60g grated Parmesan cheese
- Salt and black pepper, to taste

**Preparation instructions:**
1. Preheat the Air Fryer to 200°C for 5 minutes.
2. In a bowl, toss the broccoli florets with olive oil and minced garlic until well coated.
3. Place the coated broccoli florets in the Air Fryer basket in a single layer.
4. Air fry the Garlic Parmesan Air-Fried Broccoli Florets at 200°C for 10-12 minutes or until they are tender and slightly browned.
5. Sprinkle the grated Parmesan cheese over the broccoli florets and air fry for an additional 1-2 minutes until the cheese is melted.
6. Season with salt and black pepper to taste.
7. Once cooked, let the broccoli florets cool for a few minutes before serving.

## Pesto and Mozzarella Air-Fried Portobello Mushrooms

**Serves: 4**
**Prep time: 15 minutes / Cook time: 12 minutes**

**Ingredients:**
- 4 large Portobello mushrooms, stems removed
- 60g pesto sauce
- 100g fresh mozzarella, sliced
- 1 tbsp balsamic glaze (optional)
- Fresh basil leaves, for garnish
- Salt and black pepper, to taste

**Preparation instructions:**
1. Preheat the Air Fryer to 200°C for 5 minutes.
2. Place the Portobello mushrooms in a bowl and season with salt and black pepper.
3. Spread pesto sauce evenly on the inside of each mushroom cap.
4. Top each mushroom with slices of fresh mozzarella.
5. Place the stuffed Portobello mushrooms in the Air Fryer basket.
6. Air fry the Pesto and Mozzarella Air-Fried Portobello Mushrooms at 200°C for 10-12 minutes or until the cheese is melted and bubbly.
7. Drizzle balsamic glaze (if using) over the mushrooms and garnish with fresh basil leaves.
8. Once cooked, let the stuffed Portobello mushrooms cool for a few minutes before serving.

## Spicy Sriracha Air-Fried Green Beans

**Serves: 4**
**Prep time: 10 minutes / Cook time: 12 minutes**

**Ingredients:**
- 400g fresh green beans, trimmed
- 2 tbsp olive oil
- 2 tbsp Sriracha sauce
- 1 tsp garlic powder
- 1/2 tsp onion powder
- Salt and black pepper, to taste
- Toasted sesame seeds, for garnish (optional)

**Preparation instructions:**
1. Preheat the Air Fryer to 190°C for 5 minutes.
2. In a bowl, toss the trimmed green beans with olive oil until well coated.
3. Mix in the Sriracha sauce, garlic powder, onion powder, salt, and black pepper, and toss to coat the green beans evenly.
4. Place the seasoned green beans in the Air Fryer basket in a single layer.
5. Air fry the Spicy Sriracha Air-Fried Green Beans at 190°C for 10-12 minutes or until they are tender and slightly crispy.
6. Garnish with toasted sesame seeds, if desired.
7. Once cooked, let the green beans cool for a few minutes before serving.

## Lemon Rosemary Air-Fried Artichoke Hearts

**Serves:** 4
**Prep time:** 10 minutes / **Cook time:** 12 minutes

### Ingredients:
- 400g canned artichoke hearts, drained
- 2 tbsp olive oil
- Zest of 1 lemon
- 1 tsp dried rosemary
- Salt and black pepper, to taste
- Fresh parsley, for garnish

### Preparation instructions:
1. Preheat the Air Fryer to 200°C for 5 minutes.
2. In a bowl, toss the drained artichoke hearts with olive oil until well coated.
3. Sprinkle the lemon zest, dried rosemary, salt, and black pepper over the artichoke hearts and toss to coat evenly.
4. Place the seasoned artichoke hearts in the Air Fryer basket in a single layer.
5. Air fry the Lemon Rosemary Air-Fried Artichoke Hearts at 200°C for 10-12 minutes or until they are crispy and lightly browned.
6. Garnish with fresh parsley.
7. Once cooked, let the artichoke hearts cool for a few minutes before serving.

## Crispy Turmeric Air-Fried Okra

**Serves:** 4
**Prep time:** 10 minutes / **Cook time:** 12 minutes

### Ingredients:
- 400g fresh okra, trimmed and sliced
- 2 tbsp olive oil
- 1 tsp turmeric powder
- 1/2 tsp paprika
- 1/4 tsp cayenne pepper (optional)
- Salt and black pepper, to taste

### Preparation instructions:
1. Preheat the Air Fryer to 200°C for 5 minutes.
2. In a bowl, toss the trimmed and sliced okra with olive oil until well coated.
3. Sprinkle the turmeric powder, paprika, cayenne pepper (if using), salt, and black pepper over the okra and toss to coat evenly.
4. Place the seasoned okra in the Air Fryer basket in a single layer.
5. Air fry the Crispy Turmeric Air-Fried Okra at 200°C for 10-12 minutes or until they are crispy and lightly browned.
6. Once cooked, let the okra cool for a few minutes before serving.

## Greek Yoghurt and Herb Marinated Air-Fried Veggie Kebabs

**Serves:** 4
**Prep time:** 20 minutes / **Cook time:** 12 minutes

### Ingredients:
- 200g cherry tomatoes
- 200g button mushrooms
- 1 red pepper, cut into chunks
- 1 yellow pepper, cut into chunks
- 1 green pepper, cut into chunks
- 1 red onion, cut into chunks
- 200g courgette (courgette), cut into chunks

**For the marinade:**
- 150g Greek yoghurt
- 2 tbsp olive oil
- 1 tbsp lemon juice
- 2 garlic cloves, minced
- 2 tbsp chopped fresh parsley
- 1 tbsp chopped fresh oregano
- 1/2 tsp dried thyme
- Salt and black pepper, to taste
- Wooden skewers, soaked in water

### Preparation instructions:
1. Preheat the Air Fryer to 200°C for 5 minutes.
2. In a bowl, whisk together the Greek yoghurt, olive oil, lemon juice, minced garlic, chopped fresh parsley, chopped fresh oregano, dried thyme, salt, and black pepper to make the marinade.
3. Thread the cherry tomatoes, button mushrooms, red pepper, yellow pepper, green pepper, red onion, and courgette onto the soaked wooden skewers.
4. Place the vegetable skewers in a dish and coat them with the marinade, making sure they are evenly coated.
5. Place the vegetable skewers in the Air Fryer basket in a single layer.
6. Air fry the Greek Yoghurt and Herb Marinated Air-Fried Veggie Kebabs at 200°C for 10-12 minutes or until the vegetables are tender and slightly charred.
7. Once cooked, let the veggie kebabs cool for a few minutes before serving.

## Ranch and Bacon Air-Fried Cauliflower Tots

**Serves:** 4
**Prep time:** 15 minutes / **Cook time:** 15 minutes

### Ingredients:
- 400g cauliflower florets
- 60g cooked and crumbled bacon
- 30g grated Parmesan cheese
- 1 tbsp dried parsley

- 1 tsp onion powder
- 1/2 tsp garlic powder
- 1/2 tsp dried dill
- Salt and black pepper, to taste

**For the ranch dip:**
- 120g Greek yoghurt
- 1 tbsp dried chives
- 1 tsp dried dill
- 1 tsp onion powder
- 1 tsp garlic powder
- Salt and black pepper, to taste

### Preparation instructions:

1. Preheat the Air Fryer to 200°C for 5 minutes.
2. In a food processor, pulse the cauliflower florets until they resemble fine crumbs.
3. In a bowl, mix together the cauliflower crumbs, crumbled bacon, grated Parmesan cheese, dried parsley, onion powder, garlic powder, dried dill, salt, and black pepper to make the tots mixture.
4. Shape the tots mixture into small tots and place them in the Air Fryer basket in a single layer.
5. Air fry the Ranch and Bacon Air-Fried Cauliflower Tots at 200°C for 12-15 minutes or until they are crispy and golden brown.
6. For the ranch dip, mix together the Greek yoghurt, dried chives, dried dill, onion powder, garlic powder, salt, and black pepper in a small bowl.
7. Once cooked, serve the cauliflower tots with the ranch dip.

## Teriyaki Glazed Air-Fried Bok Choy

**Serves: 4**
**Prep time: 10 minutes / Cook time: 10 minutes**

### Ingredients:
- 4 baby bok choy, halved
- 2 tbsp soy sauce
- 2 tbsp mirin
- 1 tbsp honey
- 1 tbsp rice vinegar
- 1 tsp grated fresh ginger
- 1 garlic clove, minced
- 1 tbsp sesame seeds, for garnish
- 2 green onions, sliced, for garnish

### Preparation instructions:

1. Preheat the Air Fryer to 190°C for 5 minutes.
2. In a small bowl, whisk together the soy sauce, mirin, honey, rice vinegar, grated fresh ginger, and minced garlic to make the teriyaki glaze.
3. Place the halved baby bok choy in a dish and brush them with the teriyaki glaze, making sure they are evenly coated.
4. Place the bok choy in the Air Fryer basket in a single layer.
5. Air fry the Teriyaki Glazed Air-Fried Bok Choy at 190°C for 8-10 minutes or until they are tender and slightly charred.
6. Garnish with sesame seeds and sliced green onions.
7. Once cooked, let the bok choy cool for a few minutes before serving.

## Italian Herb Air-Fried Tomato Bruschetta

**Serves: 4**
**Prep time: 10 minutes / Cook time: 5 minutes**

### Ingredients:
- 4 ripe tomatoes, diced
- 2 garlic cloves, minced
- 2 tbsp chopped fresh basil
- 2 tbsp chopped fresh parsley
- 2 tbsp balsamic vinegar
- 2 tbsp olive oil
- Salt and black pepper, to taste
- 8 slices of baguette or ciabatta bread

### Preparation instructions:

1. Preheat the Air Fryer to 200°C for 5 minutes.
2. In a bowl, mix together the diced tomatoes, minced garlic, chopped fresh basil, chopped fresh parsley, balsamic vinegar, olive oil, salt, and black pepper to make the bruschetta topping.
3. Lightly brush the slices of baguette or ciabatta bread with olive oil.
4. Place the bread slices in the Air Fryer basket in a single layer.
5. Air fry the Italian Herb Air-Fried Tomato Bruschetta at 200°C for 3-5 minutes or until the bread is crispy and lightly toasted.
6. Top each bread slice with the tomato bruschetta mixture.
7. Once cooked, serve the Air-Fried Tomato Bruschetta immediately.

## Sweet Potato and Black Bean Air-Fried Taquitos

**Serves: 4**
**Prep time: 15 minutes / Cook time: 12 minutes**

### Ingredients:
- 400g sweet potatoes, peeled and diced
- 200g canned black beans, drained and rinsed
- 1 tsp ground cumin
- 1/2 tsp chilli powder
- 1/4 tsp garlic powder
- Salt and black pepper, to taste
- 8 small flour tortillas

- 60ml salsa, for serving
- Fresh coriander, for garnish

**Preparation instructions:**
1. Preheat the Air Fryer to 200°C for 5 minutes.
2. In a bowl, mix together the diced sweet potatoes, black beans, ground cumin, chilli powder, garlic powder, salt, and black pepper.
3. Place the sweet potato and black bean mixture in the Air Fryer basket in a single layer.
4. Air fry the Sweet Potato and Black Bean Air-Fried Taquitos at 200°C for 10-12 minutes or until the sweet potatoes are tender and lightly crispy.
5. Warm the flour tortillas in the microwave or on a griddle.
6. Place a spoonful of the sweet potato and black bean mixture on each tortilla and roll it tightly into a taquito.
6. Once cooked, serve the taquitos with salsa and garnish with fresh coriander.

## Sesame Ginger Air-Fried Snow Peas

**Serves: 4**
**Prep time: 5 minutes / Cook time: 8 minutes**

### Ingredients:
- 300g snow peas, trimmed
- 2 tbsp soy sauce
- 1 tbsp sesame oil
- 1 tbsp rice vinegar
- 1 tsp grated fresh ginger
- 1 tsp honey
- 1 tbsp sesame seeds
- Salt and black pepper, to taste

**Preparation instructions:**
1. Preheat the Air Fryer to 200°C for 5 minutes.
2. In a bowl, mix together the soy sauce, sesame oil, rice vinegar, grated fresh ginger, honey, sesame seeds, salt, and black pepper to make the sesame ginger sauce.
3. Place the trimmed snow peas in the Air Fryer basket in a single layer.
4. Air fry the Sesame Ginger Air-Fried Snow Peas at 200°C for 6-8 minutes or until they are tender-crisp.
5. Drizzle the sesame ginger sauce over the snow peas and toss to coat them evenly.
6. Once cooked, let the sesame ginger snow peas cool for a few minutes before serving.

## Balsamic Glazed Air-Fried Beet Chips

**Serves: 4**
**Prep time: 15 minutes / Cook time: 15 minutes**

### Ingredients:
- 400g beets, peeled and thinly sliced
- 2 tbsp olive oil
- 2 tbsp balsamic vinegar
- 1 tsp dried thyme
- Salt and black pepper, to taste

**Preparation instructions:**
1. Preheat the Air Fryer to 180°C for 5 minutes.
2. In a bowl, toss the thinly sliced beets with olive oil, balsamic vinegar, dried thyme, salt, and black pepper until well coated.
3. Place the coated beet slices in the Air Fryer basket in a single layer.
4. Air fry the Balsamic Glazed Air-Fried Beet Chips at 180°C for 12-15 minutes or until they are crispy and slightly caramelised.
5. Once cooked, let the beet chips cool for a few minutes before serving.

## Moroccan Spiced Air-Fried Carrot Falafel

**Serves: 4**
**Prep time: 20 minutes / Cook time: 10 minutes**

### Ingredients:
- 400g carrots, peeled and grated
- 200g canned chickpeas, drained and rinsed
- 2 garlic cloves, minced
- 2 tbsp chopped fresh coriander
- 2 tbsp chopped fresh parsley
- 1 tsp ground cumin
- 1/2 tsp ground coriander
- 1/4 tsp ground cinnamon
- 1/4 tsp ground ginger
- Salt and black pepper, to taste
- 2 tbsp olive oil

**Preparation instructions:**
1. Preheat the Air Fryer to 200°C for 5 minutes.
2. In a food processor, pulse the grated carrots, chickpeas, minced garlic, chopped fresh coriander, chopped fresh parsley, ground cumin, ground coriander, ground cinnamon, ground ginger, salt, and black pepper until well combined.
3. Shape the carrot falafel mixture into small patties and place them in the Air Fryer basket in a single layer.
4. Brush the carrot falafel patties with olive oil.
5. Air fry the Moroccan Spiced Air-Fried Carrot Falafel at 200°C for 8-10 minutes or until they are golden brown and crispy on the outside.
6. Once cooked, let the carrot falafel cool for a few minutes before serving.

## Zesty Lemon Dill Air-Fried Cabbage Wedges

**Serves: 4**
**Prep time: 10 minutes / Cook time: 12 minutes**

**Ingredients:**
- 1 small green cabbage, cut into 4 wedges
- 2 tbsp olive oil
- Zest of 1 lemon
- 1 tbsp fresh dill, chopped
- Salt and black pepper, to taste

**Preparation instructions:**
1. Preheat the Air Fryer to 190°C for 5 minutes.
2. In a bowl, toss the cabbage wedges with olive oil until well coated.
3. Sprinkle the lemon zest, chopped fresh dill, salt, and black pepper over the cabbage wedges and toss to coat evenly.
4. Place the seasoned cabbage wedges in the Air Fryer basket.
5. Air fry the Zesty Lemon Dill Air-Fried Cabbage Wedges at 190°C for 10-12 minutes or until they are tender and slightly charred.
6. Once cooked, let the cabbage wedges cool for a few minutes before serving.

## Indian Spiced Air-Fried Okra Pakoras

**Serves: 4**
**Prep time: 15 minutes / Cook time: 10 minutes**

**Ingredients:**
- 400g fresh okra, trimmed and sliced
- 100g chickpea flour
- 2 tbsp rice flour
- 1 tsp ground cumin
- 1/2 tsp ground coriander
- 1/2 tsp garam masala
- 1/4 tsp turmeric powder
- 1/4 tsp chilli powder (optional)
- 1/2 tsp baking powder
- Salt and black pepper, to taste
- 180ml water
- 2 tbsp vegetable oil

**Preparation instructions:**
1. Preheat the Air Fryer to 200°C for 5 minutes.
2. In a bowl, mix together the chickpea flour, rice flour, ground cumin, ground coriander, garam masala, turmeric powder, chilli powder (if using), baking powder, salt, and black pepper.
3. Gradually add the water to the dry Ingredients and mix until a smooth batter forms.
4. Dip the sliced okra into the batter, making sure they are well coated.
5. Place the battered okra slices in the Air Fryer basket in a single layer.
6. Drizzle the vegetable oil over the battered okra slices.
7. Air fry the Indian Spiced Air-Fried Okra Pakoras at 200°C for 8-10 minutes or until they are crispy and golden brown.
8. Once cooked, let the okra pakoras cool for a few minutes before serving.

## Spinach and Feta Stuffed Air-Fried Portobello Caps

**Serves: 4**
**Prep time: 15 minutes / Cook time: 12 minutes**

**Ingredients:**
- 4 large Portobello mushroom caps
- 200g fresh spinach, chopped
- 100g feta cheese, crumbled
- 1 garlic clove, minced
- 1 tbsp olive oil
- Salt and black pepper, to taste

**Preparation instructions:**
1. Preheat the Air Fryer to 180°C for 5 minutes.
2. In a pan, sauté the chopped spinach and minced garlic in olive oil until the spinach is wilted.
3. Season the sautéed spinach with salt and black pepper.
4. Stuff each Portobello mushroom cap with the sautéed spinach and crumbled feta cheese.
5. Place the stuffed Portobello caps in the Air Fryer basket.
6. Air fry the Spinach and Feta Stuffed Air-Fried Portobello Caps at 180°C for 10-12 minutes or until the mushrooms are tender and the cheese is melted and slightly browned.
7. Once cooked, let the stuffed Portobello caps cool for a few minutes before serving.

## Turmeric Cauliflower Rice Air-Fried Fritters

**Serves: 4**
**Prep time: 15 minutes / Cook time: 10 minutes**

**Ingredients:**
- 400g cauliflower rice
- 2 eggs, lightly beaten
- 2 tbsp chickpea flour
- 1/2 tsp ground turmeric
- 1/2 tsp ground cumin
- 1/4 tsp chilli powder (optional)
- 2 tbsp chopped fresh coriander
- Salt and black pepper, to taste
- 2 tbsp vegetable oil

**Preparation instructions:**
1. Preheat the Air Fryer to 200°C for 5 minutes.
2. In a bowl, mix together the cauliflower rice, lightly beaten eggs, chickpea flour, ground turmeric, ground cumin, chilli powder (if using), chopped fresh coriander, salt, and black pepper until well combined.
3. Shape the cauliflower rice mixture into small fritters and place them in the Air Fryer basket in a

single layer.
4. Drizzle the vegetable oil over the cauliflower rice fritters.
5. Air fry the Turmeric Cauliflower Rice Air-Fried Fritters at 200°C for 8-10 minutes or until they are crispy and lightly browned.
6. Once cooked, let the cauliflower rice fritters cool for a few minutes before serving.

## Cumin and Paprika Air-Fried Butternut Squash Cubes

**Serves: 4**
**Prep time: 15 minutes / Cook time: 15 minutes**

### Ingredients:
- 500g butternut squash, peeled and diced
- 2 tbsp olive oil
- 1 tsp ground cumin
- 1 tsp sweet paprika
- 1/2 tsp garlic powder
- Salt and black pepper, to taste

### Preparation instructions:
1. Preheat the Air Fryer to 200°C for 5 minutes.
2. In a bowl, toss the diced butternut squash with olive oil until well coated.
3. Sprinkle the ground cumin, sweet paprika, garlic powder, salt, and black pepper over the butternut squash and toss to coat evenly.
4. Place the seasoned butternut squash cubes in the Air Fryer basket in a single layer.
5. Air fry the Cumin and Paprika Air-Fried Butternut Squash Cubes at 200°C for 12-15 minutes or until they are tender and lightly caramelised.
6. Once cooked, let the butternut squash cubes cool for a few minutes before serving.

## Spicy Ranch Air-Fried Green Bean Fries

**Serves: 4**
**Prep time: 10 minutes / Cook time: 10 minutes**

### Ingredients:
- 300g fresh green beans, trimmed
- 2 tbsp olive oil
- 1 tsp garlic powder
- 1/2 tsp paprika
- 1/4 tsp cayenne pepper (optional)
- Salt and black pepper, to taste
- 60g ranch dressing, for serving

### Preparation instructions:
1. Preheat the Air Fryer to 200°C for 5 minutes.
2. In a bowl, toss the trimmed green beans with olive oil until well coated.
3. Sprinkle the garlic powder, paprika, cayenne pepper (if using), salt, and black pepper over the green beans and toss to coat evenly.
4. Place the seasoned green beans in the Air Fryer basket in a single layer.
5. Air fry the Spicy Ranch Air-Fried Green Bean Fries at 200°C for 8-10 minutes or until they are tender-crisp and slightly charred.
6. Once cooked, let the green bean fries cool for a few minutes before serving.
7. Serve with ranch dressing for dipping.

## Coconut Lime Air-Fried Sweet Potato Medallions

**Serves: 4**
**Prep time: 15 minutes / Cook time: 12 minutes**

### Ingredients:
- 500g sweet potatoes, peeled and sliced into medallions
- 2 tbsp coconut oil, melted
- Zest of 1 lime
- 1 tbsp lime juice
- 1/2 tsp ground cumin
- 1/4 tsp ground coriander
- Salt and black pepper, to taste
- 2 tbsp shredded coconut, toasted (optional)

### Preparation instructions:
1. Preheat the Air Fryer to 180°C for 5 minutes.
2. In a bowl, mix together the melted coconut oil, lime zest, lime juice, ground cumin, ground coriander, salt, and black pepper.
3. Toss the sweet potato medallions in the coconut oil mixture until well coated.
4. Place the coated sweet potato medallions in the Air Fryer basket in a single layer.
5. Air fry the Coconut Lime Air-Fried Sweet Potato Medallions at 180°C for 10-12 minutes or until they are tender and lightly crispy.
6. Sprinkle the toasted shredded coconut over the sweet potato medallions, if desired.
7. Once cooked, let the sweet potato medallions cool for a few minutes before serving.

## Hawaiian Pineapple Teriyaki Air-Fried Vegetable Skewers

**Serves: 4**
**Prep time: 20 minutes / Cook time: 10 minutes**

### Ingredients:
- 1 red pepper, cut into chunks
- 1 yellow pepper, cut into chunks
- 1 green pepper, cut into chunks
- 1 red onion, cut into chunks
- 200g pineapple chunks
- 60ml teriyaki sauce
- 1 tbsp vegetable oil

- Salt and black pepper, to taste
- 4 wooden or metal skewers

**Preparation instructions:**
1. Preheat the Air Fryer to 200°C for 5 minutes.
2. In a bowl, toss the pepper chunks, red onion chunks, and pineapple chunks with teriyaki sauce and vegetable oil until well coated.
3. Thread the marinated vegetables and pineapple onto the skewers, alternating the colours.
4. Place the vegetable skewers in the Air Fryer basket.
5. Air fry the Hawaiian Pineapple Teriyaki Air-Fried Vegetable Skewers at 200°C for 8-10 minutes or until the vegetables are tender and slightly charred.
6. Once cooked, let the vegetable skewers cool for a few minutes before serving.

## Air Fryer Roasted Brussels Sprouts with Balsamic Glaze

Serves 4
**Prep time: 10 minutes / Cook Time: 15 minutes**

### Ingredients:
- 500g Brussels sprouts, trimmed and halved
- 1 tablespoon olive oil
- 1/2 teaspoon garlic powder
- 1/2 teaspoon smoked paprika
- 1/2 teaspoon salt
- 1/4 teaspoon black pepper
- 1/4 cup balsamic vinegar
- 2 tablespoons honey
- 1 tablespoon Dijon mustard

### Preparation Instructions
1. Preheat the air fryer to 200°C (400°F).
2. In a bowl, mix the Brussels sprouts, olive oil, garlic powder, smoked paprika, salt, and black pepper.
3. Place the Brussels sprouts in the air fryer basket and cook for 10 minutes.
4. In a small bowl, whisk together the balsamic vinegar, honey, and Dijon mustard.
5. After 10 minutes, remove the Brussels sprouts from the air fryer and toss them with the balsamic glaze.
6. Return the Brussels sprouts to the air fryer and cook for an additional 5 minutes, or until they are tender and caramelized.

## Air-fried stuffed peppers with quinoa and vegetables

Serves 4
**Prep time: 15 minutes / Cook time: 25 minutes**

### Ingredients:
- 4 medium-sized bell peppers
- 185g cooked quinoa
- 75g diced zucchini
- 75g diced yellow squash
- 80g diced red onion
- 75g diced red bell pepper
- 2 cloves garlic, minced
- 2 tbsp olive oil
- 1 tsp salt
- 1/2 tsp black pepper
- 56g shredded cheddar cheese

### Preparation Instructions:
1. Preheat the air fryer to 375°F (190°C).
2. Cut off the tops of the bell peppers and remove the seeds and membranes from the inside.
3. In a large bowl, mix together the cooked quinoa, zucchini, yellow squash, red onion, red bell pepper, garlic, olive oil, salt, and black pepper.
4. Stuff the mixture into the bell peppers and place them in the air fryer basket.
5. Air fry for 20-25 minutes or until the peppers are tender and the filling is hot.
6. Remove the peppers from the air fryer and sprinkle with shredded cheddar cheese.
7. Return the peppers to the air fryer and air fry for an additional 2-3 minutes or until the cheese is melted and bubbly

## Air-fried Brussels sprouts with bacon

Serves 2
**Prep time: 10 minutes / Cook time: 15 minutes**

### Ingredients:
- 400g Brussels sprouts, trimmed and halved
- 4 slices bacon, chopped
- 2 cloves garlic, minced
- 1 tbsp olive oil
- 1/2 tsp salt
- 1/4 tsp black pepper
- 1 tbsp grated parmesan cheese

### Preparation Instructions:
1. Preheat the air fryer to 375°F (190°C).
2. In a large bowl, toss together the Brussels sprouts, bacon, garlic, olive oil, salt, and black pepper.
3. Place the mixture in the air fryer basket.
4. Air fry for 12-15 minutes or until the Brussels sprouts are crispy and the bacon is cooked.
5. Remove the Brussels sprouts and bacon from the air fryer and sprinkle with grated parmesan cheese.
6. Serve hot and enjoy!

# Chapter 7: Rice and Pasta

## Crispy Parmesan Garlic Air-Fried Risotto Balls

**Serves: 4**
**Prep time: 20 minutes / Cook time: 12 minutes**

### Ingredients:
- 300g cooked risotto (cooled and chilled)
- 50g grated Parmesan cheese
- 2 cloves garlic, minced
- 2 large eggs, beaten
- 100g breadcrumbs
- Salt and black pepper, to taste
- 2 tbsp vegetable oil

### Preparation instructions:
1. Preheat the Air Fryer to 200°C for 5 minutes.
2. In a large bowl, mix together the chilled risotto, grated Parmesan cheese, minced garlic, salt, and black pepper until well combined.
3. Take a small portion of the risotto mixture and form it into a ball. Repeat with the remaining mixture.
4. Dip each risotto ball into the beaten eggs, then roll it in breadcrumbs to coat evenly.
5. Place the coated risotto balls in the Air Fryer basket in a single layer.
6. Drizzle the vegetable oil over the risotto balls.
7. Air fry the Crispy Parmesan Garlic Air-Fried Risotto Balls at 200°C for 10-12 minutes or until they are golden brown and crispy.
8. Once cooked, let the risotto balls cool for a few minutes before serving.

## Pesto and Mozzarella Air-Fried Arancini

**Serves: 4**
**Prep time: 20 minutes / Cook time: 12 minutes**

### Ingredients:
- 300g cooked risotto (cooled and chilled)
- 50g mozzarella cheese, cut into small cubes
- 2 tbsp basil pesto
- 2 large eggs, beaten
- 100g breadcrumbs
- Salt and black pepper, to taste
- 2 tbsp vegetable oil

### Preparation instructions:
1. Preheat the Air Fryer to 200°C for 5 minutes.
2. In a large bowl, mix together the chilled risotto, basil pesto, salt, and black pepper until well combined.
3. Take a small portion of the risotto mixture and flatten it in your palm.
4. Place a mozzarella cheese cube in the centre of the flattened risotto and shape the risotto around it to form a ball. Repeat with the remaining mixture and cheese.
5. Dip each arancini ball into the beaten eggs, then roll it in breadcrumbs to coat evenly.
6. Place the coated arancini balls in the Air Fryer basket in a single layer.
7. Drizzle the vegetable oil over the arancini balls.
8. Air fry the Pesto and Mozzarella Air-Fried Arancini at 200°C for 10-12 minutes or until they are golden brown and the cheese is melted.
9. Once cooked, let the arancini balls cool for a few minutes before serving.

## Lemon Herb Air-Fried Orzo with Roasted Vegetables

**Serves: 4**
**Prep time: 15 minutes / Cook time: 15 minutes**

### Ingredients:
- 200g orzo pasta
- 400g mixed roasted vegetables (e.g., courgette, peppers, cherry tomatoes)
- 2 tbsp olive oil
- Zest of 1 lemon
- 2 tbsp lemon juice
- 2 tbsp chopped fresh parsley
- 2 tbsp chopped fresh basil
- Salt and black pepper, to taste

### Preparation instructions:
1. Preheat the Air Fryer to 180°C for 5 minutes.
2. Cook the orzo pasta according to the package instructions until al dente. Drain and set aside.
3. In a bowl, toss the mixed roasted vegetables with olive oil, salt, and black pepper.
4. Place the seasoned roasted vegetables in the Air Fryer basket.
5. Air fry the vegetables at 180°C for 10-12 minutes or until they are tender and slightly charred.
6. In a large bowl, mix together the cooked orzo pasta, lemon zest, lemon juice, chopped fresh parsley, chopped fresh basil, salt, and black pepper.
7. Add the roasted vegetables to the orzo mixture and toss until well combined.
8. Once cooked, let the Lemon Herb Air-Fried Orzo with Roasted Vegetables cool for a few minutes before serving.

## Coconut Curry Air-Fried Vegetable Fried Rice

**Serves: 4**
**Prep time: 20 minutes / Cook time: 15 minutes**

### Ingredients:

- 300g cooked basmati rice (cooled and chilled)
- 200g mixed vegetables (e.g., peas, carrots, corn, peppers)
- 1 tbsp vegetable oil
- 1 tbsp curry powder
- 200ml coconut milk
- Salt and black pepper, to taste
- 2 tbsp chopped fresh coriander

### Preparation instructions:

1. Preheat the Air Fryer to 200°C for 5 minutes.
2. In a pan, heat the vegetable oil over medium heat and sauté the mixed vegetables until they are tender-crisp.
3. Sprinkle the curry powder over the sautéed vegetables and toss to coat evenly.
4. Add the cooked basmati rice to the pan and stir-fry with the vegetables and curry powder until well combined.
5. Pour the coconut milk over the rice and vegetables, and mix until the rice is coated with the coconut curry sauce.
6. Place the coconut curry fried rice in the Air Fryer basket.
7. Air fry the Coconut Curry Air-Fried Vegetable Fried Rice at 200°C for 12-15 minutes or until it is heated through and slightly crispy on the edges.
8. Once cooked, let the coconut curry fried rice cool for a few minutes before serving.
9. Garnish with chopped fresh coriander before serving.

## Stuffed Italian Air-Fried Peppers with Tomato Rice

**Serves: 4**
**Prep time: 20 minutes / Cook time: 15 minutes**

### Ingredients:

- 4 large peppers (any colour), tops removed and seeds removed
- 200g cooked long-grain rice (cooled and chilled)
- 100g canned diced tomatoes
- 1 tsp dried oregano
- 1 tsp dried basil
- Salt and black pepper, to taste
- 50g shredded mozzarella cheese

### Preparation instructions:

1. Preheat the Air Fryer to 180°C for 5 minutes.
2. In a bowl, mix together the cooked long-grain rice, canned diced tomatoes (with the liquid), dried oregano, dried basil, salt, and black pepper.
3. Stuff each pepper with the tomato rice mixture, pressing it down gently to fill the peppers.
4. Sprinkle shredded mozzarella cheese on top of each stuffed pepper.
5. Place the stuffed peppers in the Air Fryer basket.
6. Air fry the Stuffed Italian Air-Fried Peppers with Tomato Rice at 180°C for 12-15 minutes or until the peppers are tender and the cheese is melted and slightly browned.
7. Once cooked, let the stuffed peppers cool for a few minutes before serving.

## Teriyaki Glazed Air-Fried Pineapple Rice

**Serves: 4**
**Prep time: 15 minutes / Cook time: 15 minutes**

### Ingredients:

- 300g cooked jasmine rice (cooled and chilled)
- 200g pineapple chunks
- 60ml teriyaki sauce
- 2 tbsp vegetable oil
- Salt and black pepper, to taste
- 2 spring onions, sliced
- 1 tbsp sesame seeds

### Preparation instructions:

1. Preheat the Air Fryer to 200°C for 5 minutes.
2. In a bowl, toss the pineapple chunks with teriyaki sauce and vegetable oil until well coated.
3. Place the teriyaki-glazed pineapple chunks in the Air Fryer basket in a single layer.
4. Air fry the Teriyaki Glazed Air-Fried Pineapple Rice at 200°C for 8-10 minutes or until the pineapple is caramelised and slightly charred.
5. In a separate bowl, mix together the cooked jasmine rice, salt, and black pepper.
6. Add the teriyaki-glazed pineapple chunks to the jasmine rice and toss until well combined.
7. Once cooked, let the Teriyaki Glazed Air-Fried Pineapple Rice cool for a few minutes before serving.
8. Garnish with sliced spring onions and sesame seeds before serving.

## Cheesy Garlic Air-Fried Gnocchi with Pesto

**Serves: 4**
**Prep time: 15 minutes / Cook time: 15 minutes**

### Ingredients:

- 500g potato gnocchi
- 2 tbsp olive oil
- 4 cloves garlic, minced
- 50g grated Parmesan cheese
- 60ml basil pesto
- Salt and black pepper, to taste

### Preparation instructions:

1. Preheat the Air Fryer to 200°C for 5 minutes.
2. In a large bowl, toss the potato gnocchi with olive oil, minced garlic, salt, and black pepper until well coated.
3. Place the seasoned gnocchi in the Air Fryer basket in a single layer.
4. Air fry the Cheesy Garlic Air-Fried Gnocchi with Pesto at 200°C for 12-15 minutes or until the gnocchi is golden brown and crispy.

5. Once cooked, transfer the gnocchi to a serving dish and sprinkle the grated Parmesan cheese over it.
6. Drizzle the basil pesto over the gnocchi.
7. Toss the gnocchi with the cheese and pesto until well combined.
8. Once cooked, let the Cheesy Garlic Air-Fried Gnocchi with Pesto cool for a few minutes before serving.

## Moroccan Spiced Air-Fried Cauliflower Rice Pilaf

**Serves: 4**
**Prep time: 15 minutes / Cook time: 12 minutes**

### Ingredients:
- 1 small cauliflower, grated into rice-like texture
- 1 tbsp olive oil
- 1 tsp ground cumin
- 1/2 tsp ground coriander
- 1/2 tsp ground cinnamon
- 1/2 tsp ground turmeric
- Salt and black pepper, to taste
- 50g dried cranberries
- 2 tbsp chopped fresh parsley
- 2 tbsp chopped fresh mint

### Preparation instructions:
1. Preheat the Air Fryer to 180°C for 5 minutes.
2. In a bowl, toss the grated cauliflower with olive oil, ground cumin, ground coriander, ground cinnamon, ground turmeric, salt, and black pepper until well coated.
3. Place the seasoned cauliflower rice in the Air Fryer basket.
4. Air fry the Moroccan Spiced Air-Fried Cauliflower Rice Pilaf at 180°C for 10-12 minutes or until it is cooked through and slightly crispy.
5. Once cooked, transfer the cauliflower rice to a serving dish and stir in the dried cranberries, chopped fresh parsley, and chopped fresh mint.
6. Once cooked, let the Moroccan Spiced Air-Fried Cauliflower Rice Pilaf cool for a few minutes before serving.

## Buffalo Cauliflower and Blue Cheese Air-Fried Macaroni Cups

**Serves: 4**
**Prep time: 20 minutes / Cook time: 15 minutes**

### Ingredients:
- 200g macaroni pasta
- 200g cauliflower florets
- 60ml buffalo sauce
- 50g blue cheese, crumbled
- 2 large eggs, beaten
- 100g breadcrumbs
- Salt and black pepper, to taste
- 2 tbsp vegetable oil

### Preparation instructions:
1. Preheat the Air Fryer to 200°C for 5 minutes.
2. Cook the macaroni pasta according to the package instructions until al dente. Drain and set aside.
3. In a pan, steam the cauliflower florets until they are tender.
4. In a large bowl, mix together the cooked macaroni pasta, steamed cauliflower, buffalo sauce, crumbled blue cheese, salt, and black pepper.
5. Take a small portion of the macaroni mixture and press it into a silicone muffin cup to form a cup shape. Repeat with the remaining mixture.
6. Dip each macaroni cup into the beaten eggs, then roll it in breadcrumbs to coat evenly. Place the coated macaroni cups in the Air Fryer basket in a single layer.
7. Drizzle the vegetable oil over the macaroni cups.
8. Air fry the Buffalo Cauliflower and Blue Cheese Air-Fried Macaroni Cups at 200°C for 12-15 minutes or until they are golden brown and crispy.
9. Once cooked, let the macaroni cups cool for a few minutes before serving.

## Coconut Lime Air-Fried Jasmine Rice Balls

**Serves: 4**
**Prep time: 20 minutes / Cook time: 12 minutes**

### Ingredients:
- 300g cooked jasmine rice (cooled and chilled)
- 50g desiccated coconut
- Zest of 1 lime
- 60ml coconut milk
- 2 tbsp sugar
- Salt, to taste

### Preparation instructions:
1. Preheat the Air Fryer to 200°C for 5 minutes.
2. In a large bowl, mix together the cooked jasmine rice, desiccated coconut, lime zest, coconut milk, sugar, and salt until well combined.
3. Take a small portion of the rice mixture and form it into a ball. Repeat with the remaining mixture.
4. Place the rice balls in the Air Fryer basket in a single layer.
5. Air fry the Coconut Lime Air-Fried Jasmine Rice Balls at 200°C for 10-12 minutes or until they are golden brown and slightly crispy.
6. Once cooked, let the rice balls cool for a few minutes before serving.

# Chapter 8: Appetisers and Snacks

## Coconut Curry Air-Fried Brussels Sprouts

**Serves: 4**
**Prep time: 10 minutes / Cook time: 15 minutes**

**Ingredients:**

- 400g Brussels sprouts, halved
- 2 tbsp coconut oil, melted
- 1 tsp curry powder
- 1/2 tsp turmeric powder
- 1/4 tsp cayenne pepper (optional for heat)
- Salt and black pepper, to taste
- Lime wedges, for serving

**Preparation instructions:**

1. Preheat the Air Fryer to 200°C for 5 minutes.
2. In a large bowl, toss the halved Brussels sprouts with melted coconut oil, curry powder, turmeric powder, cayenne pepper (if using), salt, and black pepper until well coated.
3. Place the seasoned Brussels sprouts in the Air Fryer basket in a single layer.
4. Air fry the Coconut Curry Air-Fried Brussels Sprouts at 200°C for 10-12 minutes or until they are tender and slightly crispy.
5. Once cooked, remove from the Air Fryer and serve with lime wedges on the side.

## Crispy Carrot Parmesan Fries

**Serves: 4**
**Prep time: 15 minutes / Cook time: 12 minutes**

**Ingredients:**

- 4 large Carrots, cut into thin strips
- 60g grated Parmesan cheese
- 50g breadcrumbs
- 1 tsp garlic powder
- 1 tsp onion powder
- 1/2 tsp dried oregano
- 1/2 tsp dried basil
- Salt and black pepper, to taste
- 2 large eggs, beaten

**Preparation instructions:**

1. Preheat the Air Fryer to 200°C for 5 minutes.
2. In a shallow dish, mix together the grated Parmesan cheese, breadcrumbs, garlic powder, onion powder, dried oregano, dried basil, salt, and black pepper.
3. Dip each carrot strip into the beaten eggs, then coat it with the Parmesan mixture.
4. Place the coated carrot strips in the Air Fryer basket in a single layer.
5. Air fry the Crispy carrot Parmesan Fries at 200°C for 10-12 minutes or until they are golden brown and crispy.
6. Once cooked, remove from the Air Fryer and serve immediately.

## Lemon Herb Air-Fried Asparagus Spears

**Serves: 4**
**Prep time: 10 minutes / Cook time: 8 minutes**

**Ingredients:**

- 400g asparagus spears, trimmed
- 2 tbsp olive oil
- Zest of 1 lemon
- 2 cloves garlic, minced
- 1 tsp dried thyme
- 1 tsp dried rosemary
- Salt and black pepper, to taste
- Lemon wedges, for serving

**Preparation instructions:**

1. Preheat the Air Fryer to 200°C for 5 minutes.
2. In a bowl, toss the trimmed asparagus spears with olive oil, lemon zest, minced garlic, dried thyme, dried rosemary, salt, and black pepper until well coated.
3. Place the seasoned asparagus spears in the Air Fryer basket in a single layer.
4. Air fry the Lemon Herb Air-Fried Asparagus Spears at 200°C for 6-8 minutes or until they are tender-crisp.
5. Once cooked, remove from the Air Fryer and serve with lemon wedges on the side.

## Cajun Shrimp and Sausage Air-Fried Jambalaya Bites

**Serves: 4**
**Prep time: 15 minutes / Cook time: 15 minutes**

**Ingredients:**

- 200g cooked shrimp, peeled and deveined
- 200g cooked sausage (e.g., Andouille or smoked sausage), chopped
- 200g cooked rice
- 1 tbsp Cajun seasoning
- 1 tsp paprika
- 1/2 tsp dried thyme
- 1/4 tsp cayenne pepper (optional for heat)

- Salt and black pepper, to taste
- 2 large eggs, beaten
- 100g breadcrumbs

**Preparation instructions:**
1. Preheat the Air Fryer to 200°C for 5 minutes.
2. In a large bowl, mix together the cooked shrimp, chopped sausage, cooked rice, Cajun seasoning, paprika, dried thyme, cayenne pepper (if using), salt, and black pepper until well combined.
3. Form the mixture into bite-sized balls.
4. Dip each jambalaya bite into the beaten eggs, then roll it in breadcrumbs to coat evenly.
5. Place the coated jambalaya bites in the Air Fryer basket in a single layer.
6. Air fry the Cajun Shrimp and Sausage Air-Fried Jambalaya Bites at 200°C for 12-15 minutes or until they are golden brown and crispy.
7. Once cooked, remove from the Air Fryer and serve immediately.

## Mediterranean Stuffed Air-Fried Grape Leaves

**Serves: 4**
**Prep time: 20 minutes / Cook time: 12 minutes**

### Ingredients:
- 200g jarred grape leaves, drained and rinsed
- 100g cooked quinoa
- 100g crumbled feta cheese
- 50g chopped black olives
- 50g chopped sun-dried tomatoes
- 2 tbsp chopped fresh parsley
- 2 tbsp chopped fresh dill
- 2 tbsp lemon juice
- 2 tbsp olive oil
- Salt and black pepper, to taste

### Preparation instructions:
1. Preheat the Air Fryer to 200°C for 5 minutes.
2. In a bowl, mix together the cooked quinoa, crumbled feta cheese, chopped black olives, chopped sun-dried tomatoes, chopped fresh parsley, chopped fresh dill, lemon juice, olive oil, salt, and black pepper.
3. Lay out a grape leaf, shiny side down, and place a spoonful of the quinoa mixture in the centre.
4. Fold the sides of the grape leaf over the filling, then roll it up tightly to form a stuffed grape leaf.
5. Repeat with the remaining grape leaves and quinoa mixture.
6. Place the stuffed grape leaves in the Air Fryer basket in a single layer.
7. Air fry the Mediterranean Stuffed Air-Fried Grape Leaves at 200°C for 8-10 minutes or until they are heated through and slightly crispy.
8. Once cooked, remove from the Air Fryer and serve immediately.

## Pesto and Mozzarella Air-Fried Arancini

**Serves: 4**
**Prep time: 20 minutes / Cook time: 12 minutes**

### Ingredients:
- 200g cooked risotto, cooled and chilled
- 60g mozzarella cheese, cut into small cubes
- 2 tbsp basil pesto
- 2 large eggs, beaten
- 100g breadcrumbs
- 2 tbsp olive oil

### Preparation instructions:
1. Preheat the Air Fryer to 200°C for 5 minutes.
2. Take a small portion of the cooled risotto and flatten it in your palm.
3. Place a mozzarella cheese cube in the centre, then top it with a small dollop of basil pesto.
4. Fold the risotto around the cheese and pesto to form a ball. Repeat with the remaining risotto, cheese, and pesto.
5. Dip each arancini ball into the beaten eggs, then roll it in breadcrumbs to coat evenly.
6. Place the coated arancini balls in the Air Fryer basket in a single layer.
7. Drizzle the olive oil over the arancini balls.
8. Air fry the Pesto and Mozzarella Air-Fried Arancini at 200°C for 10-12 minutes or until they are golden brown and crispy.
9. Once cooked, let the arancini balls cool for a few minutes before serving.

## Tex-Mex Air-Fried Chicken and Rice Taquitos

**Serves: 4**
**Prep time: 20 minutes / Cook time: 12 minutes**

### Ingredients:
- 200g cooked chicken, shredded
- 100g cooked rice
- 100g black beans, drained and rinsed
- 100g corn kernels (fresh, canned, or frozen)
- 1 tsp chilli powder
- 1/2 tsp ground cumin
- 1/4 tsp garlic powder
- Salt and black pepper, to taste
- 8 small flour tortillas

- 2 large eggs, beaten
- 100g breadcrumbs
- Vegetable oil, for brushing

**Preparation instructions:**
1. Preheat the Air Fryer to 200°C for 5 minutes.
2. In a bowl, mix together the shredded chicken, cooked rice, black beans, corn kernels, chilli powder, ground cumin, garlic powder, salt, and black pepper until well combined.
3. Lay out a flour tortilla and place a spoonful of the chicken and rice mixture on one end.
4. Roll up the tortilla tightly to form a taquito. Repeat with the remaining tortillas and filling.
5. Dip each taquito into the beaten eggs, then roll it in breadcrumbs to coat evenly.
6. Place the coated taquitos in the Air Fryer basket in a single layer.
7. Brush the tops of the taquitos with vegetable oil.
8. Air fry the Tex-Mex Air-Fried Chicken and Rice Taquitos at 200°C for 10-12 minutes or until they are golden brown and crispy.
9. Once cooked, remove from the Air Fryer and serve immediately.

## Spinach and Feta Stuffed Air-Fried Portobello Caps

**Serves: 4**
**Prep time: 15 minutes / Cook time: 12 minutes**

**Ingredients:**
- 4 large Portobello mushroom caps, stems removed
- 200g frozen spinach, thawed and drained
- 100g crumbled feta cheese
- 2 cloves garlic, minced
- 2 tbsp chopped fresh parsley
- 2 tbsp chopped fresh dill
- 1 tbsp olive oil
- Salt and black pepper, to taste

**Preparation instructions:**
1. Preheat the Air Fryer to 200°C for 5 minutes.
2. In a bowl, mix together the thawed and drained spinach, crumbled feta cheese, minced garlic, chopped fresh parsley, chopped fresh dill, olive oil, salt, and black pepper until well combined.
3. Stuff each Portobello mushroom cap with the spinach and feta mixture.
4. Place the stuffed Portobello caps in the Air Fryer basket.
5. Air fry the Spinach and Feta Stuffed Air-Fried Portobello Caps at 200°C for 10-12 minutes or until the mushrooms are tender and the filling is heated through.
6. Once cooked, remove from the Air Fryer and serve immediately.

## Zesty Lemon Dill Air-Fried Cabbage Wedges

**Serves: 4**
**Prep time: 10 minutes / Cook time: 12 minutes**

**Ingredients:**
- 1 medium green cabbage, cut into wedges
- 2 tbsp olive oil
- Zest of 1 lemon
- 2 tbsp lemon juice
- 2 cloves garlic, minced
- 1 tbsp chopped fresh dill
- Salt and black pepper, to taste

**Preparation instructions:**
1. Preheat the Air Fryer to 200°C for 5 minutes.
2. In a bowl, mix together the olive oil, lemon zest, lemon juice, minced garlic, chopped fresh dill, salt, and black pepper.
3. Brush the cabbage wedges with the lemon dill mixture, coating them evenly.
4. Place the seasoned cabbage wedges in the Air Fryer basket.
5. Air fry the Zesty Lemon Dill Air-Fried Cabbage Wedges at 200°C for 10-12 minutes or until they are tender-crisp and slightly charred.
6. Once cooked, remove from the Air Fryer and serve immediately.

## Hawaiian Pineapple Teriyaki Air-Fried Butter Beans

**Serves: 4**
**Prep time: 10 minutes / Cook time: 12 minutes**

**Ingredients:**
- 400g canned butter beans, drained and rinsed
- 100g pineapple chunks (fresh, canned, or frozen)
- 60ml teriyaki sauce
- 1 tbsp honey
- 1/2 tsp ground ginger
- 1/4 tsp garlic powder
- Salt and black pepper, to taste
- 2 tbsp chopped fresh coriander (coriander), for garnish

**Preparation instructions:**
1. Preheat the Air Fryer to 200°C for 5 minutes.
2. In a bowl, mix together the butter beans, pineapple chunks, teriyaki sauce, honey, ground ginger, garlic

powder, salt, and black pepper until well coated.
3. Place the seasoned butter beans and pineapple in the Air Fryer basket.
4. Air fry the Hawaiian Pineapple Teriyaki Air-Fried Butter Beans at 200°C for 10-12 minutes or until the beans are heated through and slightly caramelised.
5. Once cooked, remove from the Air Fryer, garnish with chopped fresh coriander, and serve immediately.

## Garlic Parmesan Air-Fried Green Bean Fries

**Serves: 4**
**Prep time: 10 minutes / Cook time: 12 minutes**

### Ingredients:
- 200g fresh green beans, trimmed
- 2 tbsp olive oil
- 2 cloves garlic, minced
- 60g grated Parmesan cheese
- 2 tbsp breadcrumbs
- Salt and black pepper, to taste

### Preparation instructions:
1. Preheat the Air Fryer to 200°C for 5 minutes.
2. In a bowl, toss the trimmed green beans with olive oil and minced garlic until well coated.
3. In a separate bowl, mix together the grated Parmesan cheese, breadcrumbs, salt, and black pepper.
4. Dip each green bean into the Parmesan mixture, coating them evenly.
5. Place the coated green bean fries in the Air Fryer basket.
6. Air fry the Garlic Parmesan Air-Fried Green Bean Fries at 200°C for 8-10 minutes or until they are crispy and golden brown.
7. Once cooked, remove from the Air Fryer and serve immediately.

## Indian Spiced Air-Fried Okra Pakoras

**Serves: 4**
**Prep time: 15 minutes / Cook time: 12 minutes**

### Ingredients:
- 200g fresh okra, sliced
- 100g chickpea flour (gram flour)
- 2 tbsp rice flour
- 1 tsp ground cumin
- 1/2 tsp ground coriander
- 1/2 tsp garam masala
- 1/4 tsp chilli powder (adjust to taste)
- 1/4 tsp baking powder
- Salt, to taste
- 150ml water
- Vegetable oil, for brushing

### Preparation instructions:
1. Preheat the Air Fryer to 200°C for 5 minutes.
2. In a bowl, mix together the chickpea flour, rice flour, ground cumin, ground coriander, garam masala, chilli powder, baking powder, and salt.
3. Gradually add water to the flour mixture and whisk until you get a smooth and thick batter.
4. Dip the sliced okra into the batter, coating them evenly.
5. Place the coated okra pakoras in the Air Fryer basket in a single layer.
6. Brush the pakoras with vegetable oil to enhance crispiness.
7. Air fry the Indian Spiced Air-Fried Okra Pakoras at 200°C for 10-12 minutes or until they are golden and crispy.
8. Once cooked, remove from the Air Fryer and serve immediately.

## Ranch and Bacon Air-Fried Cauliflower Tots

**Serves: 4**
**Prep time: 15 minutes / Cook time: 12 minutes**

### Ingredients:
- 400g cauliflower florets, finely chopped
- 60g grated cheddar cheese
- 2 tbsp chopped fresh chives
- 2 large eggs, beaten
- 50g breadcrumbs
- 1 tbsp ranch seasoning mix
- Salt and black pepper, to taste
- 4 rashers of bacon, cooked and crumbled

### Preparation instructions:
1. Preheat the Air Fryer to 200°C for 5 minutes.
2. In a bowl, mix together the finely chopped cauliflower, grated cheddar cheese, chopped fresh chives, beaten eggs, breadcrumbs, ranch seasoning mix, salt, and black pepper.
3. Form the mixture into tots or small cylindrical shapes.
4. Place the cauliflower tots in the Air Fryer basket in a single layer.
5. Air fry the Ranch and Bacon Air-Fried Cauliflower Tots at 200°C for 10-12 minutes or until they are golden brown and crispy.
6. Once cooked, remove from the Air Fryer, sprinkle with crumbled bacon, and serve immediately.

# Lemon Rosemary Air-Fried Artichoke Hearts

**Serves: 4**
**Prep time: 10 minutes / Cook time: 12 minutes**

### Ingredients:

- 400g canned artichoke hearts, drained and patted dry
- 2 tbsp olive oil
- Zest of 1 lemon
- 2 tbsp lemon juice
- 2 cloves garlic, minced
- 1 tbsp chopped fresh rosemary
- Salt and black pepper, to taste

### Preparation instructions:

1. Preheat the Air Fryer to 200°C for 5 minutes.
2. In a bowl, mix together the artichoke hearts, olive oil, lemon zest, lemon juice, minced garlic, chopped fresh rosemary, salt, and black pepper until well coated.
3. Place the seasoned artichoke hearts in the Air Fryer basket.
4. Air fry the Lemon Rosemary Air-Fried Artichoke Hearts at 200°C for 10-12 minutes or until they are heated through and slightly crispy.
5. Once cooked, remove from the Air Fryer and serve immediately.

# Buffalo Cauliflower and Blue Cheese Air-Fried Macaroni Cups

**Serves: 4**
**Prep time: 15 minutes / Cook time: 15 minutes**

### Ingredients:

- 200g cauliflower florets, finely chopped
- 100g macaroni pasta, cooked
- 60ml buffalo hot sauce
- 60ml milk
- 50g crumbled blue cheese
- 50g grated cheddar cheese
- 1 large egg, beaten
- Salt and black pepper, to taste
- 2 tbsp chopped fresh chives, for garnish

### Preparation instructions:

1. Preheat the Air Fryer to 200°C for 5 minutes.
2. In a bowl, mix together the finely chopped cauliflower, cooked macaroni pasta, buffalo hot sauce, milk, crumbled blue cheese, grated cheddar cheese, beaten egg, salt, and black pepper until well combined.
3. Divide the mixture evenly among 4 silicone muffin cups.
4. Place the muffin cups in the Air Fryer basket.
5. Air fry the Buffalo Cauliflower and Blue Cheese Air-Fried Macaroni Cups at 200°C for 12-15 minutes or until they are set and slightly golden brown on top.
6. Once cooked, remove from the Air Fryer, garnish with chopped fresh chives, and serve immediately.

# Coconut Lime Air-Fried Sweet Potato Medallions

**Serves: 4**
**Prep time: 15 minutes / Cook time: 15 minutes**

### Ingredients:

- 400g sweet potatoes, peeled and sliced into medallions
- 2 tbsp coconut oil, melted
- Zest of 1 lime
- 1 tbsp lime juice
- 1/2 tsp ground cumin
- 1/2 tsp ground coriander
- Salt and black pepper, to taste
- 2 tbsp chopped fresh coriander, for garnish

### Preparation instructions:

1. Preheat the Air Fryer to 200°C for 5 minutes.
2. In a bowl, mix together the melted coconut oil, lime zest, lime juice, ground cumin, ground coriander, salt, and black pepper.
3. Toss the sweet potato medallions in the coconut lime mixture until well coated.
4. Place the seasoned sweet potato medallions in the Air Fryer basket.
5. Air fry the Coconut Lime Air-Fried Sweet Potato Medallions at 200°C for 12-15 minutes or until they are tender and slightly crispy.
6. Once cooked, remove from the Air Fryer, garnish with chopped fresh coriander, and serve immediately.

# Stuffed Italian Air-Fried Peppers with Tomato Rice

**Serves: 4**
**Prep time: 20 minutes / Cook time: 20 minutes**

### Ingredients:

- 4 large peppers (any colour), tops removed and seeds removed
- 200g cooked rice
- 400g canned chopped tomatoes
- 1 tbsp tomato paste
- 1 clove garlic, minced
- 1/2 tsp dried oregano
- 1/2 tsp dried basil
- Salt and black pepper, to taste
- 100g grated mozzarella cheese

- 2 tbsp chopped fresh parsley, for garnish

**Preparation instructions:**

1. Preheat the Air Fryer to 180°C for 5 minutes.
2. In a bowl, mix together the cooked rice, canned chopped tomatoes, tomato paste, minced garlic, dried oregano, dried basil, salt, and black pepper.
3. Stuff each pepper with the tomato rice mixture.
4. Place the stuffed peppers in the Air Fryer basket.
5. Air fry the Stuffed Italian Air-Fried Peppers with Tomato Rice at 180°C for 18-20 minutes or until the peppers are tender and slightly charred.
6. In the last 2 minutes of cooking, top each stuffed pepper with grated mozzarella cheese and allow it to melt.
7. Once cooked, remove from the Air Fryer, garnish with chopped fresh parsley, and serve immediately.

## Moroccan Spiced Air-Fried Carrot Falafel

Serves: 4
**Prep time: 20 minutes / Cook time: 15 minutes**

### Ingredients:

- 400g carrots, peeled and grated
- 1 can (400g) chickpeas, drained and rinsed
- 2 cloves garlic, minced
- 2 tbsp chopped fresh coriander (coriander)
- 2 tbsp chopped fresh parsley
- 1 tsp ground cumin
- 1/2 tsp ground coriander
- 1/2 tsp ground cinnamon
- 1/4 tsp ground ginger
- 1/4 tsp ground paprika
- 1/4 tsp cayenne pepper (adjust to taste)
- 2 tbsp chickpea flour (gram flour)
- Salt and black pepper, to taste
- 2 tbsp olive oil, for brushing

**Preparation instructions:**

1. Preheat the Air Fryer to 200°C for 5 minutes.
2. In a food processor, combine the grated carrots, chickpeas, minced garlic, chopped fresh coriander, chopped fresh parsley, ground cumin, ground coriander, ground cinnamon, ground ginger, ground paprika, cayenne pepper, chickpea flour, salt, and black pepper. Pulse until well combined, but not completely smooth.
3. Form the carrot falafel mixture into small patties.
4. Place the carrot falafel patties in the Air Fryer basket.
5. Brush the falafel patties with olive oil to enhance crispiness.
6. Air fry the Moroccan Spiced Air-Fried Carrot Falafel at 200°C for 12-15 minutes or until they are golden brown and crispy.
7. Once cooked, remove from the Air Fryer and serve immediately.

## Caprese Air-Fried Ravioli Skewers

Serves: 4
**Prep time: 15 minutes / Cook time: 12 minutes**

### Ingredients:

- 200g fresh cheese ravioli
- 12 cherry tomatoes
- 100g mozzarella balls (bocconcini)
- 2 tbsp olive oil
- 1 tbsp balsamic vinegar
- 2 tbsp chopped fresh basil
- Salt and black pepper, to taste
- Wooden skewers

**Preparation instructions:**

1. Preheat the Air Fryer to 200°C for 5 minutes.
2. Cook the cheese ravioli according to the package instructions, then drain and let them cool slightly.
3. In a bowl, mix together the cooked cheese ravioli, cherry tomatoes, mozzarella balls, olive oil, balsamic vinegar, chopped fresh basil, salt, and black pepper until well coated.
4. Thread the ravioli, cherry tomatoes, and mozzarella balls onto the wooden skewers alternately.
5. Place the skewers in the Air Fryer basket.
6. Air fry the Caprese Air-Fried Ravioli Skewers at 200°C for 10-12 minutes or until the ravioli are crispy and the mozzarella is melted.
7. Once cooked, remove from the Air Fryer and serve immediately.

## Balsamic Glazed Air-Fried Beet Chips

Serves: 4
**Prep time: 15 minutes / Cook time: 12 minutes**

### Ingredients:

- 400g fresh beets, peeled and thinly sliced
- 2 tbsp olive oil
- 2 tbsp balsamic vinegar
- 1/2 tsp dried thyme
- Salt and black pepper, to taste

**Preparation instructions:**

1. Preheat the Air Fryer to 200°C for 5 minutes.
2. In a bowl, mix together the thinly sliced beets, olive oil, balsamic vinegar, dried thyme, salt, and

black pepper until well coated.
3. Place the seasoned beet slices in the Air Fryer basket.
4. Air fry the Balsamic Glazed Air-Fried Beet Chips at 200°C for 10-12 minutes or until they are crispy and slightly caramelised.
5. Once cooked, remove from the Air Fryer and serve immediately.

## Cajun Air-Fried Black Eyed Peas

**Serves: 4**
**Prep time: 10 minutes / Cook time: 15 minutes**

### Ingredients:
- 400g canned black-eyed peas, drained and rinsed
- 2 tbsp olive oil
- 1 tsp Cajun seasoning
- 1/2 tsp garlic powder
- 1/2 tsp onion powder
- 1/4 tsp cayenne pepper (adjust to taste)
- Salt and black pepper, to taste

### Preparation instructions:
1. Preheat the Air Fryer to 200°C for 5 minutes.
2. In a bowl, mix together the black-eyed peas, olive oil, Cajun seasoning, garlic powder, onion powder, cayenne pepper, salt, and black pepper until well coated.
3. Place the seasoned black-eyed peas in the Air Fryer basket.
4. Air fry the Cajun Air-Fried Black Eyed Peas at 200°C for 12-15 minutes or until they are crispy and slightly browned.
5. Once cooked, remove from the Air Fryer and serve immediately.

## Lemon Poppy Seed Air-Fried Donut Holes

**Serves: 4**
**Prep time: 10 minutes / Cook time: 8 minutes**

### Ingredients:
- 100g all-purpose flour
- 50g granulated sugar
- 1 tsp baking powder
- 1/4 tsp salt
- 2 tbsp melted butter
- 60ml milk
- 1 large egg
- Zest of 1 lemon
- 1 tbsp poppy seeds
- 50g powdered sugar, for dusting
- 1 tbsp lemon juice

### Preparation instructions:
1. Preheat the Air Fryer to 180°C for 5 minutes.
2. In a bowl, whisk together the all-purpose flour, granulated sugar, baking powder, and salt.
3. In a separate bowl, mix together the melted butter, milk, egg, lemon zest, and poppy seeds.
4. Combine the wet and dry Ingredients, stirring until just combined.
5. Form small balls of dough (donut holes) and place them in the Air Fryer basket.
6. Air fry the Lemon Poppy Seed Air-Fried Donut Holes at 180°C for 8 minutes or until they are golden brown and cooked through.
7. In a shallow bowl, mix together the powdered sugar and lemon juice to make the glaze.
8. Once the donut holes are cooked, remove from the Air Fryer and dip them in the lemon glaze.
9. Serve the Lemon Poppy Seed Air-Fried Donut Holes immediately.

## Crispy Parmesan Garlic Air-Fried Risotto Balls

**Serves: 4**
**Prep time: 15 minutes / Cook time: 15 minutes**

### Ingredients:
- 300g cooked risotto rice
- 50g grated Parmesan cheese
- 2 cloves garlic, minced
- 1 tbsp chopped fresh parsley
- 1/2 tsp dried oregano
- 1/4 tsp dried thyme
- Salt and black pepper, to taste
- 2 large eggs, beaten
- 100g breadcrumbs
- 2 tbsp olive oil, for brushing

### Preparation instructions:
1. Preheat the Air Fryer to 200°C for 5 minutes.
2. In a bowl, mix together the cooked risotto rice, grated Parmesan cheese, minced garlic, chopped fresh parsley, dried oregano, dried thyme, salt, and black pepper.
3. Form the risotto mixture into small balls and place them on a plate.
4. Dip each risotto ball into the beaten eggs, then roll in breadcrumbs until well coated.
5. Place the coated risotto balls in the Air Fryer basket.
6. Brush the risotto balls with olive oil to enhance crispiness.
7. Air fry the Crispy Parmesan Garlic Air-Fried

Risotto Balls at 200°C for 12-15 minutes or until they are golden brown and crispy.
8. Once cooked, remove from the Air Fryer and serve immediately.

# Indian Spiced Air-Fried Lentil Samosas

**Serves: 4**
**Prep time: 20 minutes / Cook time: 15 minutes**

## Ingredients:
- 200g cooked lentils (any variety), mashed
- 1 small onion, finely chopped
- 1 clove garlic, minced
- 1 tsp grated fresh ginger
- 1/2 tsp ground cumin
- 1/2 tsp ground coriander
- 1/4 tsp ground turmeric
- 1/4 tsp garam masala
- 1/4 tsp cayenne pepper (adjust to taste)
- Salt, to taste
- 2 tbsp chopped fresh coriander (coriander)
- 8 sheets of spring roll pastry (or filo pastry), cut into triangles
- 2 tbsp olive oil, for brushing

## Preparation instructions:
1. Preheat the Air Fryer to 200°C for 5 minutes.
2. In a bowl, mix together the mashed lentils, finely chopped onion, minced garlic, grated fresh ginger, ground cumin, ground coriander, ground turmeric, garam masala, cayenne pepper, salt, and chopped fresh coriander.
3. Place a spoonful of the lentil mixture in the centre of each pastry triangle.
4. Fold the pastry over the filling to form a triangle shape and seal the edges using a little water.
5. Place the lentil samosas in the Air Fryer basket.
6. Brush the samosas with olive oil to enhance crispiness.
7. Air fry the Indian Spiced Air-Fried Lentil Samosas at 200°C for 12-15 minutes or until they are golden brown and crispy.
8. Once cooked, remove from the Air Fryer and serve immediately.

# Hawaiian Pineapple Teriyaki Air-Fried Rice Crackers

**Serves: 4**
**Prep time: 10 minutes / Cook time: 15 minutes**

## Ingredients:
- 100g rice crackers
- 60ml teriyaki sauce
- 50g diced pineapple
- 2 spring onions, thinly sliced
- 1 tbsp sesame seeds
- 1 tbsp chopped fresh coriander

## Preparation instructions:
1. Preheat the Air Fryer to 180°C for 5 minutes.
2. In a bowl, mix together the rice crackers, teriyaki sauce, diced pineapple, and thinly sliced spring onions until the crackers are well coated.
3. Place the teriyaki-coated rice crackers in the Air Fryer basket.
4. Air fry the Hawaiian Pineapple Teriyaki Air-Fried Rice Crackers at 180°C for 12-15 minutes or until the crackers are crispy and the teriyaki sauce has caramelised slightly.
5. Once cooked, remove from the Air Fryer, sprinkle with sesame seeds and chopped fresh coriander, and serve immediately.

# Chapter 9: Desserts

## Cinnamon Sugar Air-Fried Apple Fritters

**Serves: 4**
**Prep time: 15 minutes / Cook time: 10 minutes**

### Ingredients:
- 200g all-purpose flour
- 50g granulated sugar
- 1 tsp baking powder
- 1/4 tsp salt
- 1/2 tsp ground cinnamon
- 120ml milk
- 1 large egg
- 1 tsp vanilla extract
- 2 medium apples, peeled, cored, and diced
- Vegetable oil, for brushing
- Cinnamon sugar mixture (2 tbsp sugar + 1 tsp ground cinnamon) for coating

### Preparation instructions:
1. Preheat the Air Fryer to 180°C for 5 minutes.
2. In a bowl, whisk together the all-purpose flour, granulated sugar, baking powder, salt, and ground cinnamon.
3. In a separate bowl, whisk together the milk, egg, and vanilla extract.
4. Gradually add the wet Ingredients to the dry Ingredients, stirring until just combined.
5. Gently fold in the diced apples.
6. Brush the Air Fryer basket with vegetable oil to prevent sticking.
7. Drop spoonfuls of the apple fritter batter into the Air Fryer basket, making sure to leave space between them.
8. Air fry the Cinnamon Sugar Air-Fried Apple Fritters at 180°C for 8-10 minutes or until they are golden brown and cooked through.
9. Once cooked, remove from the Air Fryer and immediately coat each fritter in the cinnamon sugar mixture. Let the fritters cool for a few minutes before serving.

## S'mores Air-Fried Empanadas

**Serves: 4**
**Prep time: 15 minutes / Cook time: 12 minutes**

### Ingredients:
- 200g pie crust dough (store-bought or homemade)
- 16 mini marshmallows
- 16 chocolate chips (milk or dark chocolate)
- 4 tbsp graham cracker crumbs
- 1 large egg, beaten
- 2 tbsp granulated sugar

### Preparation instructions:
1. Preheat the Air Fryer to 180°C for 5 minutes.
2. Roll out the pie crust dough on a lightly floured surface and cut it into circles (approximately 10 cm in diameter).
3. Place 4 mini marshmallows and 4 chocolate chips on one half of each dough circle.
4. Sprinkle 1 tablespoon of graham cracker crumbs over the marshmallows and chocolate. Fold the other half of the dough circle over the filling to form a half-moon shape.
5. Use a fork to press and seal the edges of the empanadas.
6. Brush the empanadas with beaten egg and sprinkle granulated sugar on top.
7. Place the empanadas in the Air Fryer basket.
8. Air fry the S'mores Air-Fried Empanadas at 180°C for 10-12 minutes or until they are golden brown and crispy.
9. Once cooked, remove from the Air Fryer and let cool for a few minutes before serving.

## Red Velvet Air-Fried Whoopie Pies

**Serves: 4**
**Prep time: 20 minutes / Cook time: 10 minutes**

### Ingredients:
**For the cookies:**
- 150g all-purpose flour
- 20g cocoa powder
- 1/2 tsp baking powder
- 1/4 tsp baking soda
- 1/4 tsp salt
- 60ml buttermilk
- 1 tsp red food colouring
- 1 tsp vanilla extract
- 60g unsalted butter, softened
- 100g granulated sugar
- 1 large egg

**For the cream cheese filling:**
- 100g cream cheese, softened
- 50g unsalted butter, softened
- 100g powdered sugar
- 1/2 tsp vanilla extract

**Preparation instructions:**

1. Preheat the Air Fryer to 160°C for 5 minutes. In a bowl, whisk together the all-purpose flour, cocoa powder, baking powder, baking soda, and salt.
2. In a separate bowl, mix together the buttermilk, red food colouring, and vanilla extract. In another bowl, cream together the softened unsalted butter and granulated sugar until light and fluffy. Add the egg and mix until well combined.
3. Gradually add the dry Ingredients to the wet Ingredients, alternating with the buttermilk mixture, and mix until a smooth batter forms.
4. Drop spoonfuls of the red velvet batter onto a baking sheet lined with parchment paper to make 8 cookies.
5. Place the cookies in the Air Fryer basket.
6. Air fry the Red Velvet Air-Fried Whoopie Pies at 160°C for 8-10 minutes or until they are set. Once cooked, remove from the Air Fryer and let the cookies cool completely.
7. For the cream cheese filling, beat together the softened cream cheese, softened unsalted butter, powdered sugar, and vanilla extract until smooth and creamy.
8. Spread a generous amount of the cream cheese filling on the flat side of 4 cookies and sandwich them with the remaining 4 cookies.
9. Serve the Red Velvet Air-Fried Whoopie Pies immediately, or refrigerate them for a firmer filling.

# Raspberry Coconut Almond Granola Bars

**Serves: 4**
**Prep time: 15 minutes / Cook time: 12 minutes**

## Ingredients:

- 100g rolled oats
- 50g shredded coconut
- 50g almonds, chopped
- 40g dried raspberries
- 60ml honey
- 60ml almond butter
- 1 tsp vanilla extract
- A pinch of salt

## Preparation instructions:

1. Preheat the Air Fryer to 160°C for 5 minutes.
2. In a large bowl, combine the rolled oats, shredded coconut, chopped almonds, and dried raspberries.
3. In a separate microwave-safe bowl, mix together the honey, almond butter, vanilla extract, and a pinch of salt.
4. Microwave the honey mixture for 20-30 seconds until it becomes smooth and easy to pour.
5. Pour the honey mixture over the dry Ingredients and mix until everything is well combined. Line a small baking dish with parchment paper, leaving some extra paper hanging over the sides for easy removal later.
6. Press the granola mixture firmly into the baking dish, making sure it's evenly distributed. Place the baking dish in the Air Fryer basket.
7. Air fry the Raspberry Coconut Almond Granola Bars at 160°C for 10-12 minutes or until they turn slightly golden.
8. Once cooked, remove from the Air Fryer and let them cool completely in the baking dish.
9. Once cooled, lift the granola slab out of the dish using the parchment paper overhang, and cut it into bars.

# Matcha Green Tea Air-Fried Macarons

**Serves: 4**
**Prep time: 20 minutes / Cook time: 8 minutes**

## Ingredients:

**For the macaron shells:**

- 100g almond flour
- 100g powdered sugar
- 2 tsp matcha green tea powder
- 2 large egg whites
- 50g granulated sugar
- A pinch of cream of tartar

**For the filling:**

- 50g white chocolate, chopped
- 50ml heavy cream
- 1 tsp matcha green tea powder
- Matcha powder or edible gold dust for dusting (optional)

## Preparation instructions:

1. Preheat the Air Fryer to 160°C for 5 minutes.
2. In a food processor, pulse together the almond flour, powdered sugar, and matcha green tea powder until well combined.
3. In a separate bowl, beat the egg whites until frothy. Add a pinch of cream of tartar and continue beating until soft peaks form.
4. Gradually add the granulated sugar to the egg whites, a little at a time, and continue beating until stiff peaks form.
5. Gently fold the dry Ingredients into the beaten egg whites until you get a smooth, thick batter.
6. Transfer the batter to a piping bag fitted with a round tip.

7. Pipe small rounds of batter onto a baking sheet lined with parchment paper.
8. Place the baking sheet in the Air Fryer basket.
9. Air fry the Matcha Green Tea Air-Fried Macarons at 160°C for 7-8 minutes or until the macarons are set.
10. Once cooked, remove from the Air Fryer and let them cool completely on the baking sheet.
11. For the filling, heat the heavy cream in a saucepan over medium heat until it simmers.
12. Remove from heat and stir in the chopped white chocolate and matcha green tea powder until smooth and creamy.
13. Let the filling cool and thicken slightly.
14. Sandwich two cooled macaron shells together with a dollop of the matcha white chocolate filling.
15. Optionally, dust the macarons with additional matcha powder or edible gold dust for decoration.

## Cheesecake-Stuffed Air-Fried Strawberries

**Serves: 4**
**Prep time: 15 minutes / Cook time: 5 minutes**

### Ingredients:
- 16 large strawberries
- 100g cream cheese, softened
- 30g powdered sugar
- 1 tsp vanilla extract
- 50g graham cracker crumbs

### Preparation instructions:
1. Preheat the Air Fryer to 160°C for 5 minutes.
2. Wash and dry the strawberries. Cut off the tops and use a small spoon or a strawberry huller to create a hollow cavity in each strawberry.
3. In a bowl, mix together the softened cream cheese, powdered sugar, and vanilla extract until smooth and creamy.
4. Transfer the cream cheese mixture to a piping bag or a plastic sandwich bag with one corner cut off.
5. Pipe the cream cheese filling into the hollowed-out strawberries. Place the graham cracker crumbs in a shallow dish.
6. Roll each stuffed strawberry in the graham cracker crumbs to coat the filling.
7. Place the strawberries in the Air Fryer basket.
8. Air fry the Cheesecake-Stuffed Air-Fried Strawberries at 160°C for 3-5 minutes or until the strawberries are slightly softened.
9. Once cooked, remove from the Air Fryer and let them cool slightly before serving.

## Mini Berry Galettes with Air-Fried Crusts

**Serves: 4**
**Prep time: 25 minutes / Cook time: 15 minutes**

### Ingredients:
**For the crust:**
- 200g all-purpose flour
- 1 tbsp granulated sugar
- A pinch of salt
- 120g unsalted butter, cold and diced
- 60ml ice water

**For the filling:**
- 100g mixed berries (blueberries, raspberries, blackberries)
- 1 tbsp granulated sugar
- 1 tbsp cornstarch
- 1 tsp lemon juice
- 1/2 tsp lemon zest

**For assembling:**
- 1 large egg, beaten
- 1 tbsp milk
- 1 tbsp turbinado sugar (or granulated sugar)

### Preparation instructions:
1. Preheat the Air Fryer to 180°C for 5 minutes. In a food processor, pulse together the all-purpose flour, granulated sugar, and a pinch of salt.
2. Add the cold diced unsalted butter to the food processor and pulse until the mixture resembles coarse crumbs. Gradually add the ice water, a little at a time, and pulse until the dough comes together.
3. Transfer the dough to a floured surface and knead it gently to form a smooth ball.
4. Divide the dough into 4 equal portions and roll each portion into a small disc. In a bowl, mix together the mixed berries, granulated sugar, cornstarch, lemon juice, and lemon zest until well combined.
5. Place a spoonful of the berry filling in the centre of each dough disc, leaving a border around the edges. Fold the edges of the dough over the filling, partially covering it and creating a rustic galette shape.
6. In a small bowl, mix together the beaten egg and milk to create an egg wash.
7. Brush the edges of the galettes with the egg wash and sprinkle turbinado sugar over them. Place the galettes in the Air Fryer basket.
8. Air fry the Mini Berry Galettes at 180°C for 12-15 minutes or until the crusts are golden brown and the berry filling is bubbly.
9. Once cooked, remove from the Air Fryer and let them cool slightly before serving.

# Blueberry Lemon Air-Fried Pound Cake Bites

**Serves: 4**
**Prep time: 15 minutes / Cook time: 10 minutes**

## Ingredients:
- 100g pound cake, cut into small cubes
- 60g blueberries
- 1 tbsp granulated sugar
- 1 tsp lemon zest
- 1 tsp lemon juice
- Vanilla ice cream or whipped cream for serving (optional)

## Preparation instructions:
1. Preheat the Air Fryer to 180°C for 5 minutes.
2. In a bowl, gently toss together the pound cake cubes, blueberries, granulated sugar, lemon zest, and lemon juice until well coated.
3. Place the pound cake and blueberry mixture in the Air Fryer basket.
4. Air fry the Blueberry Lemon Air-Fried Pound Cake Bites at 180°C for 8-10 minutes or until the pound cake is slightly toasted and the blueberries are soft and juicy.
5. Once cooked, remove from the Air Fryer and let them cool slightly before serving.
6. Serve the Blueberry Lemon Air-Fried Pound Cake Bites with a scoop of vanilla ice cream or a dollop of whipped cream if desired.

# Oreo Air-Fried Cake Pops

**Serves: 4**
**Prep time: 20 minutes / Cook time: 5 minutes**

## Ingredients:
- 10 Oreo cookies
- 50g cream cheese, softened
- 100g white chocolate, melted
- Sprinkles or crushed Oreos for decoration (optional)
- Lollipop sticks or cake pop sticks

## Preparation instructions:
1. Preheat the Air Fryer to 160°C for 5 minutes.
2. In a food processor, pulse the Oreo cookies until they turn into fine crumbs.
3. In a bowl, mix together the Oreo crumbs and softened cream cheese until well combined.
4. Shape the mixture into small balls, about 2-3 cm in diameter.
5. Insert a lollipop stick into each Oreo cake ball.
6. Place the Oreo cake pops in the Air Fryer basket.
7. Air fry the Oreo Air-Fried Cake Pops at 160°C for 4-5 minutes or until they turn slightly golden. Once cooked, remove from the Air Fryer and let them cool slightly before handling.
8. Dip each cake pop into the melted white chocolate, and decorate with sprinkles or crushed Oreos if desired.
9. Place the dipped cake pops on a parchment-lined tray and let the chocolate set before serving.

# Chocolate Chip Cookie Dough Air-Fried Egg Rolls

**Serves: 4**
**Prep time: 20 minutes / Cook time: 5 minutes**

## Ingredients:
- 100g chocolate chip cookie dough (store-bought or homemade)
- 50g chocolate chips
- 1 large egg, beaten
- Icing sugar for dusting
- Chocolate sauce or caramel sauce for dipping (optional)

## Preparation instructions:
1. Preheat the Air Fryer to 180°C for 5 minutes.
2. Divide the chocolate chip cookie dough into 4 equal portions.
3. Flatten each portion of cookie dough into a small disc, about 2-3 cm in diameter.
4. Place a few chocolate chips in the centre of each cookie dough disc.
5. Fold the edges of the dough over the chocolate chips, sealing them inside and creating a small egg roll shape.
6. Brush the beaten egg over the outside of each cookie dough egg roll.
7. Place the cookie dough egg rolls in the Air Fryer basket.
8. Air fry the Chocolate Chip Cookie Dough Air-Fried Egg Rolls at 180°C for 4-5 minutes or until they turn golden brown. Once cooked, remove from the Air Fryer and let them cool slightly before serving.
9. Dust the egg rolls with icing sugar and serve with chocolate sauce or caramel sauce for dipping if desired.

# Pineapple Coconut Air-Fried Spring Rolls

**Serves: 4**
**Prep time: 30 minutes / Cook time: 10 minutes**

## Ingredients:
- 100g pineapple chunks, finely chopped

- 50g shredded coconut
- 30g granulated sugar
- 8 spring roll wrappers
- 1 large egg, beaten
- Vegetable oil for brushing

**Preparation instructions:**

1. Preheat the Air Fryer to 180°C for 5 minutes.
2. In a bowl, mix together the finely chopped pineapple, shredded coconut, and granulated sugar until well combined.
3. Lay a spring roll wrapper on a clean surface with one corner facing you (like a diamond shape).
4. Place a spoonful of the pineapple coconut filling in the centre of the wrapper, forming a horizontal line. Fold the bottom corner of the wrapper over the filling and roll it up tightly halfway. Fold the left and right corners of the wrapper toward the centre, and continue rolling it up tightly into a spring roll shape.
5. Brush the top corner of the wrapper with the beaten egg to seal the spring roll.
6. Repeat the process with the remaining spring roll wrappers and filling.
7. Lightly brush each spring roll with vegetable oil on all sides. Place the spring rolls in the Air Fryer basket.
8. Air fry the Pineapple Coconut Air-Fried Spring Rolls at 180°C for 8-10 minutes or until they turn crispy and golden brown. Once cooked, remove from the Air Fryer and let them cool slightly before serving.
9. Serve the Pineapple Coconut Air-Fried Spring Rolls as a delicious sweet treat.

## Chai Spiced Air-Fried Rice Pudding Cups

**Serves: 4**
**Prep time: 10 minutes / Cook time: 20 minutes**

**Ingredients:**

- 500ml whole milk
- 80g long-grain rice
- 40g granulated sugar
- 1 cinnamon stick
- 4 cardamom pods, lightly crushed
- 1/2 tsp ground ginger
- 1/4 tsp ground cloves
- 1/4 tsp ground nutmeg
- 1/4 tsp ground black pepper
- Chopped pistachios and dried rose petals for garnish (optional)

**Preparation instructions:**

1. Preheat the Air Fryer to 160°C for 5 minutes.
2. In a saucepan, combine the whole milk, long-grain rice, granulated sugar, cinnamon stick, crushed cardamom pods, ground ginger, ground cloves, ground nutmeg, and ground black pepper.
3. Bring the mixture to a boil over medium heat, stirring occasionally.
4. Once it starts boiling, reduce the heat to low and let the rice pudding simmer for about 15-20 minutes or until the rice is cooked and the pudding has thickened.
5. Remove the cinnamon stick and cardamom pods from the rice pudding.
6. Spoon the rice pudding into individual serving cups or ramekins.
7. Place the cups in the Air Fryer basket.
8. Air fry the Chai Spiced Air-Fried Rice Pudding Cups at 160°C for 5-7 minutes or until the tops turn slightly golden.
9. Once cooked, remove from the Air Fryer and let them cool slightly before serving. Garnish with chopped pistachios and dried rose petals for a delightful touch.

## Blackberry Lavender Air-Fried Tarts

**Serves: 4**
**Prep time: 25 minutes / Cook time: 15 minutes**

**Ingredients:**

**For the lavender pastry crust:**

- 200g all-purpose flour
- 2 tbsp granulated sugar
- 1 tsp dried lavender flowers (culinary grade)
- 120g unsalted butter, cold and diced
- 60ml ice water

**For the blackberry filling:**

- 200g fresh blackberries
- 2 tbsp granulated sugar
- 1 tbsp cornstarch
- 1 tsp lemon juice

**For assembling:**

- 1 large egg, beaten
- 1 tbsp milk
- 1 tbsp turbinado sugar (or granulated sugar)

**Preparation instructions:**

1. Preheat the Air Fryer to 180°C for 5 minutes. In a food processor, pulse together the all-purpose flour, granulated sugar, and dried lavender flowers.
2. Add the cold diced unsalted butter to the food processor and pulse until the mixture resembles coarse crumbs.

3. Gradually add the ice water, a little at a time, and pulse until the dough comes together. Transfer the dough to a floured surface and knead it gently to form a smooth ball.
4. Roll out the dough into a large circle and cut it into 4 equal portions.
5. In a bowl, mix together the fresh blackberries, granulated sugar, cornstarch, and lemon juice until well combined. Place a spoonful of the blackberry filling in the centre of each pastry portion.
6. Fold the edges of the pastry over the blackberry filling, partially covering it and creating a rustic tart shape. In a small bowl, mix together the beaten egg and milk to create an egg wash.
7. Brush the edges of the tarts with the egg wash and sprinkle turbinado sugar over them. Place the tarts in the Air Fryer basket.
8. Air fry the Blackberry Lavender Air-Fried Tarts at 180°C for 12-15 minutes or until the pastry crusts are golden brown and the blackberry filling is bubbly.
9. Once cooked, remove from the Air Fryer and let them cool slightly before serving. Serve the Blackberry Lavender Air-Fried Tarts as a delightful dessert.

# Mint Chocolate Chip Air-Fried Ice Cream Bites

**Serves: 4**
**Prep time: 20 minutes / Cook time: 5 minutes**

## Ingredients:
- 250g mint chocolate chip ice cream, softened
- 100g chocolate chips
- 50g crushed chocolate wafer cookies
- 1 large egg, beaten
- Icing sugar for dusting
- Chocolate sauce or mint syrup for drizzling (optional)

## Preparation instructions:
1. Preheat the Air Fryer to 180°C for 5 minutes.
2. Line a small baking dish with parchment paper.
3. Spread the softened mint chocolate chip ice cream evenly in the baking dish.
4. Sprinkle the chocolate chips and crushed chocolate wafer cookies over the ice cream, pressing them gently into the surface.
5. Place the baking dish in the freezer for about 1 hour or until the ice cream hardens again.
6. Remove the frozen ice cream from the baking dish and cut it into small bite-sized squares or balls. Place the ice cream bites in the Air Fryer basket.
7. Air fry the Mint Chocolate Chip Air-Fried Ice Cream Bites at 180°C for 3-5 minutes or until the chocolate chips and cookies turn slightly toasted.
8. Once cooked, remove from the Air Fryer and let them cool slightly before serving.
9. Dust the ice cream bites with icing sugar and drizzle with chocolate sauce or mint syrup for added indulgence.

# Caramelized Banana Air-Fried Chimichangas

**Serves: 4**
**Prep time: 15 minutes / Cook time: 10 minutes**

## Ingredients:
- 4 large flour tortillas
- 4 ripe bananas, sliced
- 2 tbsp unsalted butter, melted
- 2 tbsp granulated sugar
- 1/2 tsp ground cinnamon
- 1/4 tsp vanilla extract
- Vanilla ice cream or whipped cream for serving (optional)

## Preparation instructions:
1. Preheat the Air Fryer to 180°C for 5 minutes.
2. In a bowl, toss the sliced bananas with melted butter, granulated sugar, ground cinnamon, and vanilla extract until well coated.
3. Lay a flour tortilla on a clean surface and place a portion of the caramelised banana mixture in the centre of the tortilla.
4. Fold the sides of the tortilla over the banana mixture, then fold the bottom and top edges to form a chimichanga shape.
5. Repeat the process with the remaining tortillas and banana mixture.
6. Place the chimichangas in the Air Fryer basket.
7. Air fry the Caramelized Banana Air-Fried Chimichangas at 180°C for 8-10 minutes or until they turn crispy and golden brown.
8. Once cooked, remove from the Air Fryer and let them cool slightly before serving.
9. Serve the Caramelized Banana Air-Fried Chimichangas with a scoop of vanilla ice cream or a dollop of whipped cream if desired.

# Cannoli Air-Fried Wonton Cups

**Serves: 4**
**Prep time: 20 minutes / Cook time: 5 minutes**

## Ingredients:
- 12 wonton wrappers

- 200g ricotta cheese
- 50g powdered sugar
- 1 tsp vanilla extract
- 30g mini chocolate chips
- Icing sugar for dusting

**Preparation instructions:**

1. Preheat the Air Fryer to 160°C for 5 minutes.
2. Gently press each wonton wrapper into a muffin cup of the Air Fryer to form a cup shape.
3. In a bowl, mix together the ricotta cheese, powdered sugar, and vanilla extract until smooth.
4. Stir in the mini chocolate chips into the ricotta mixture.
5. Spoon the ricotta mixture into the wonton cups, filling them to the top.
6. Place the wonton cups in the Air Fryer basket.
7. Air fry the Cannoli Air-Fried Wonton Cups at 160°C for 3-5 minutes or until the wonton wrappers turn crispy and golden.
8. Once cooked, remove from the Air Fryer and let them cool slightly before serving.
9. Dust the Cannoli Air-Fried Wonton Cups with icing sugar before serving for an authentic touch.

## Caramel Popcorn Air-Fried Cake

**Serves: 4**
**Prep time: 15 minutes / Cook time: 20 minutes**

**Ingredients:**

- 150g unsalted butter, melted
- 100g granulated sugar
- 2 large eggs
- 150g all-purpose flour
- 1 tsp baking powder
- 1/4 tsp salt
- 50 ml whole milk
- 1 tsp vanilla extract
- 50g caramel popcorn

**Preparation instructions:**

1. Preheat the Air Fryer to 170°C for 5 minutes.
2. In a bowl, whisk together the melted butter and granulated sugar until well combined.
3. Add the eggs to the butter mixture, one at a time, mixing well after each addition.
4. In a separate bowl, sift together the all-purpose flour, baking powder, and salt.
5. Gradually add the dry Ingredients to the butter mixture, alternating with the whole milk, and mix until smooth.
6. Stir in the vanilla extract and caramel popcorn into the cake batter. Grease a small cake pan that fits inside the Air Fryer basket.
7. Pour the cake batter into the greased cake pan. Place the cake pan in the Air Fryer basket.
8. Air fry the Caramel Popcorn Air-Fried Cake at 170°C for 18-20 minutes or until a toothpick inserted in the centre comes out clean.
9. Once cooked, remove from the Air Fryer and let the cake cool slightly before serving.

## Strawberry Shortcake Air-Fried Napoleons

**Serves: 4**
**Prep time: 15 minutes / Cook time: 10 minutes**

**Ingredients:**

- 8 sheets of puff pastry, thawed
- 200ml double cream
- 2 tbsp powdered sugar
- 1 tsp vanilla extract
- 200g fresh strawberries, sliced
- Icing sugar for dusting

**Preparation instructions:**

1. Preheat the Air Fryer to 180°C for 5 minutes. Place four sheets of puff pastry on a flat surface and cut each sheet into 4 equal squares.
2. In a small bowl, whisk together the double cream, powdered sugar, and vanilla extract until soft peaks form.
3. Spread a dollop of the whipped cream on each puff pastry square.
4. Arrange a few slices of fresh strawberries on top of the whipped cream.
5. Repeat the process with another layer of puff pastry, whipped cream, and strawberries, creating a napoleon-style dessert.
6. Top the final layer with a puff pastry square and dust with icing sugar.
7. Place the napoleons in the Air Fryer basket.
8. Air fry the Strawberry Shortcake Air-Fried Napoleons at 180°C for 8-10 minutes or until the puff pastry turns golden brown and flaky.
9. Once cooked, remove from the Air Fryer and let them cool slightly before serving.

## Cinnamon Apple Air-Fried Samosas

**Serves: 4**
**Prep time: 20 minutes / Cook time: 10 minutes**

**Ingredients:**

- 4 sheets of spring roll pastry
- 2 large apples, peeled, cored, and diced
- 2 tbsp granulated sugar

- 1/2 tsp ground cinnamon
- 1/4 tsp ground nutmeg
- 1 tbsp lemon juice
- 1 tbsp cornstarch
- 1 tbsp water
- Icing sugar for dusting

**Preparation instructions:**

1. Preheat the Air Fryer to 190°C for 5 minutes.
2. In a bowl, combine the diced apples, granulated sugar, ground cinnamon, ground nutmeg, and lemon juice.
3. In a small bowl, mix the cornstarch and water to create a slurry.
4. Stir the cornstarch slurry into the apple mixture until well coated. Lay a spring roll pastry sheet on a flat surface and cut it into 3 equal strips.
5. Spoon a portion of the apple filling onto one end of each pastry strip.
6. Fold the end with the apple filling over to form a triangle, then continue folding the triangle over itself until you reach the end of the pastry strip.
7. Repeat the process with the remaining apple filling and pastry strips to make more samosas. Place the samosas in the Air Fryer basket.
8. Air fry the Cinnamon Apple Air-Fried Samosas at 190°C for 8-10 minutes or until they turn crispy and golden brown. Once cooked, remove from the Air Fryer and let them cool slightly before serving.
9. Dust the Cinnamon Apple Air-Fried Samosas with icing sugar for an extra touch of sweetness.

# Raspberry White Chocolate Air-Fried Turnovers

**Serves: 4**
**Prep time: 15 minutes / Cook time: 10 minutes**

**Ingredients:**

- 1 sheet of puff pastry, thawed
- 100g fresh raspberries
- 50g white chocolate chips
- 1 large egg, beaten
- Icing sugar for dusting

**Preparation instructions:**

1. Preheat the Air Fryer to 180°C for 5 minutes.
2. On a floured surface, roll out the puff pastry sheet to make it slightly thinner.
3. Cut the puff pastry sheet into 4 equal squares.
4. Place a few fresh raspberries and white chocolate chips on one side of each puff pastry square. Fold the other half of the puff pastry over the raspberries and chocolate to form a turnover shape.
5. Press the edges of the turnover with a fork to seal them.
6. Brush the turnovers with the beaten egg to create a golden finish.
7. Place the turnovers in the Air Fryer basket.
8. Air fry the Raspberry White Chocolate Air-Fried Turnovers at 180°C for 8-10 minutes or until the pastry turns golden brown and flaky. Once cooked, remove from the Air Fryer and let them cool slightly before serving.
9. Dust the Raspberry White Chocolate Air-Fried Turnovers with icing sugar for an elegant touch.

Printed in Great Britain
by Amazon